The TV Ritual

The
TV Ritual

Worship at the
Video Altar

Gregor T. Goethals

Beacon Press   Boston

Grateful acknowledgment is made to the following: ABC News for permission to reproduce pictures of John Paul II, the funeral services of Hubert Humphrey, and "Live from the Moon"; WNET/Thirteen for permission to reproduce a picture of John Dean; WNET for permission to quote from two WNET programs, "The Adversaries" and "The MacNeil Lehrer Report," copyright © 1974 and 1980, respectively, by the Educational Broadcasting Corporation; CBS News for permission to reproduce pictures of Walter Cronkite, Edward R. Murrow, and the *60 Minutes* logo; Tat Communications Company and Bonnie Franklin for permission to reproduce a picture of her from *One Day at a Time*; and Tandem Productions, Carroll O'Connor, and Jean Stapleton for permission to reproduce a picture of them from *All in the Family*. Photos from *Little House on the Prairie* and *Buck Rogers in the 25th Century* reproduced courtesy of The National Broadcasting Company, Inc.

Library of Congress Cataloging in Publication Data

Goethals, Gregor T   1926–
    The TV ritual.

    Includes index.
    1.   Television — Psychological aspects.   2.   Television broadcasting — Social aspects — United States.
I.   Title.
PN1992.6.G6   791.45'01'9   80–66072
ISBN 0-8070-3222-0

For my family

Acknowledgments

This book originated and developed through a process of inter-disciplinary work with humanists from a variety of disciplines. The Society for Values in Higher Education provided a network of scholars and opportunities for multidisciplinary perspectives. Directors Harry Smith and, later, David Smith put me in touch with persons interested in discussing television's role in the production of public symbols. John Maguire, president of the Society, arranged for meetings that extended these discussions to other professional groups. Presentations at these meetings and seminars resulted in two essays that Ray Browne published in the *Journal of Popular Culture*. James S. Ackerman read these and suggested they be extended and developed into a book.

Funding by Lilly Endowment, Inc., for team research on theology and popular culture at the Weston School of Theology brought me into discussions about television with members of that faculty. Conversations with Dick Clifford, Peter Fink, Leo O'Donovan, and John Padberg contributed significantly to the formation of some of the concepts used here. During this time Robert Lynn and Skip Lawrence provided thoughtful and critical reviews of the project. An important part of the research program included the photographing of television images in order to "capture" those transient forms for reflection and critical analysis.

Following this research came the opportunity to plan a public exhibition of the images photographed from television. Its purpose was to encourage persons to think about the symbolic power of television as electronic ritual, icon, and iconoclasm. Funding for the planning came from the Alexandria Museum in Alexandria, Louisiana, and from the National Endowment for the Humanities. Those responsible for organizing the exhibition were Fran Davis, Ada D. Jarred, and Hope Norman. Dai Sil Kim and Nancy Worssam made many helpful recommendations. The planning process also included the production of some television tapes. These could not have been made without the energetic and thoughtful efforts of Fred Baus, Chris Pruszynski, and Ben Pate.

The first production of the exhibition itself, *TV: America's Super Symbols*, was funded by the Rhode Island Committee for the Humanities. I am especially grateful to Tom Roberts, Fred Weber, and Malcolm Grear Associates for their work and encouragement. A similar exhibition is being funded by the Louisiana Committee for the Humanities under the sponsorship of the Alexandria Museum and Louisiana State University at Alexandria.

While chapters of the book and exhibition panels were being put together, there were invaluable communications with colleagues. I am grateful for the opportunity of teamteaching with Dick Niebuhr. Many of the ideas presented here were first developed in that setting. Throughout the writing of this book I have worked within a community of practicing artists and humanists at the Rhode Island School of Design. Dirk Back, Ned Dwyer, Jim Fowle, Barry Kirschenbaum, Tom Reed, and Cathy Seigel consistently offered the careful criticism and challenge one needs to clarify and refine ideas. To all faculty and students there I want to acknowledge my appreciation of an environment of persons who make, think, and care about images.

Karen Sullivan, Shirley Diodati, and Bonnie Gee undertook the typing and assumed responsibility for many other tasks, working often under pressured circumstances.

In developing the manuscript and exhibition design I called on a number of scholars as consultants and readers: James Luther Adams, Albert Anderson, Robert Bellah, Peter Berger, Herman Blake, David Burrell, John Cook, Roland Delattre, Diana Eck, Margaret Farley, Rhoda Flaxman, George Forrell, Daniel X. Freedman, Diana Johnson, William Lee Miller, Roberta Reeder, Bruce Rigdon, Michael Robinson, Max Stackhouse, Ruel Tyson, and George H. Williams. Discussions with them about ideas and images contributed to the formation of both the manuscript and the exhibition.

In the throes of the final drafts I turned to several persons who went through the manuscript with scrupulous care: Aidan Kavanagh, Ruth Lancaster, Paula Cooey-Nichols, Sallie McFague, Dick Niebuhr, Horace Newcomb, David Thorburn, and Connie Wentzel. Their insight and criticism enabled me to see the old ideas in a new way.

Finally, there are three persons of whom it must be said, "Without them, this book would not have come into being." MaryAnn Lash of Beacon Press encouraged me to transform early essays and exhibition ideas into a manuscript. Later, the editor, Joanne Wyckoff, worked with meticulous care on all phases of the book. Then, more than anyone else, I am indebted to Virginia Clifford who, from concepts through draft after draft, worked ceaselessly in the editing and shaping of the manuscript.

Only through a continuing process of shared reflections with friends and colleagues would this imagemaker have dared to venture into the world of words.

Gregor T. Goethals
Cambridge, Massachusetts
September 1980

Contents

Illustrations

(All photographs are courtesy of the author.)

Introduction

The electronic images of television are both persuasive and elusive. Each day thousands of these images speed past the average viewer and he or she is left with only a diffused awareness of their impact. Like the flux of experience itself, television images rush quickly by and elude our prolonged contemplation and critical analysis. What symbolic worlds have these images produced in the mind? How are social, economic, and political beliefs being communicated?

Many questions will arise in the course of this book but there is a starting question which generates the others: "How do images function in a technological society?" This question is especially compelling if we consider the roles of images in other cultures. In premodern, less differentiated cultures, particularly those prior to the late eighteenth century, images were major forms through which world views were deliberately expressed and shaped. A relatively small group of leaders selected the subjects to be represented for the larger community. The chosen images, depicting events from history or myth, gave meaning to the existence of the individual and the whole group. Because of widespread illiteracy, images were the chief instruments for social integration and community orientation. Whatever the range and degree of seriousness employed in looking at it — which must have varied from individual to individual — the image attuned persons to the totality of social experience. It was a means of knowing who one was and what the society, even the universe, was like.

Today, communities such as churches continue to provide their members with myths and visual symbols. At the same time, however, commercial television, especially as it has developed over the last twenty years, has played a major role in expressing and shaping our values. It has done so by weaving a web of easily understood and accessible images that provides fragmented groups with public symbols. In a highly complex society, television has begun to perform one of the oldest, most traditional functions of images: to visualize common myths and to integrate the individual into a social whole.

In making connections between older, more traditional forms and contemporary television, there is a need to distinguish between two levels on which television functions. The first is spelled out by the vocabulary and program structure of broadcasters, producers, and *TV Guide*. On that level, the news informs, commercials sell products, and sit-coms and sports entertain. There is, however, a much deeper level on which these images operate: all television images — news, sports, sit-coms, commercials, soap operas — provide the American public with fundamental rituals and myths. Much of what people think about the "good life," the roles of men and women, technology, or the changing patterns of family and political life emerges from the television set. On a deeper level television mediates and reinforces public symbols; it also, however, can trivialize myths and ritual, reducing them to a kind of ornate emptiness.

In reflecting on television images as mediators of societal symbols, I shall refer to two traditional forms through which meaning systems have been communicated: *icon* or "sacred image" and *ritual* or "enactment of myth." Rituals and icons provided concrete ways for each person to become attuned to the belief system of the social whole. Moreover, as anthropologists have shown, icon and ritual also played a revolutionary as well as conservative role in groups. Under certain historical and cultural conditions they effected social change organically from within the society.

Another tradition to which I will refer is *iconoclasm*. It is associated with religions that have prohibited the use of images, especially those that purport to communicate the sacred. In the ancient world, iconoclasm meant the destruction of images and of the false power they contained. Judaism and Protestantism had roots in this aniconic tradition. Protestant communities, for example, emphasized sacred scripture and the word or verbal image, rather than the visual image. In the modern world iconoclasm also refers to a stringent criticism of powers thought to be false. The images themselves are agents of change. And, with the technological innovations in photography, film, and television, iconoclasm increasingly involves the use of images to deliberately or inadvertently criticize, question, or even destroy abusive institutions.

Although my interpretation of television uses icons, rituals, and iconoclasm, television communication needs many different interpretations — from humanistic perspectives to statistical analyses. Indeed, changes in technology and regulatory legislation mean that any interpretation or study of the medium will be revised constantly. American television did not develop in an imagistic void, but has appropriated and transformed older cultural symbols. Therefore, from the visual arts I have chosen what I see as major iconic and iconoclastic motifs in American culture. Clearly my selection is a partial one. Other persons considering the meaning of television images might find different interpretative patterns. Moreover, I do not attempt to treat every type of TV program. It will be obvious that there are many — quiz and game, mystery, variety and talk shows — that might not be illumined by this approach.

All persons, whatever their educational or cultural background, tend to find fault with television for one reason or another. Few are satisfied, or so they say, with this or that kind of programming. Many people look upon TV viewing as a waste of time. One question put to me during the writing of this book was: "Why do you compare *television* with profound art forms?" My answer is that I am interested in images and their functions and television, as we know it today, seems to be a primary source of popular piety and public symbols. Although I use traditional religious art forms to interpret contemporary television, I do not wish to imply that there is a corresponding aesthetic quality or an equal profundity of world views. Icon and ritual serve primarily to clarify and emphasize the role of images in providing world views.

Underlying all aspects of this book is an anthropological and religious assumption that symbol making is one of our most fundamental human activities. I use the broad sociological definition of religion developed by Max Weber and Emile Durkheim. It was Weber who spoke of

> the metaphysical needs of the human mind as it is driven to reflect on ethical and religious questions, driven not by material need but by an inner compulsion to understand the world as a meaningful cosmos and to take up a position toward it.[1]

I also refer to the work of scholars such as Ernest Becker, Peter L. Berger, Mircea Eliade, H. Richard Niebuhr, Thomas Luckmann, and Victor Turner, who have rethought and enriched our concepts of myth and ritual. In the language and theories of Berger and Luckmann, television images embody a "symbolic universe" that shelters us from the ultimate terror of an anomic existence. These images that reach us through television may in some strange, perhaps perverse, way confirm us as basically nomic creatures. They often trade both on our own intolerance of anomie and on our capacity for diversion and escape from the confusion of everyday experience. Yet, however trivial they may seem to some, the symbols depicted on television screens become for many Americans a means of locating themselves in an ordered world. Where traditional institutions and high art do not provide meaningful public symbols, television images rush in to fill the void.

1
Ritual:
Ceremony and
Super-Sunday

From the rhythms of a Hopi rain dance to the liturgical motions of priest and communicants, ritual is a deeply rooted human activity. Studies by sociologists and anthropologists have shown how religious communities develop various forms of patterned action to put the group in touch with transcendent reality. Even those communities that disavow ritual objects and liturgy use repeated sequences of words, music, and action in their practice of worship. It is also true that the complexity of rituals does not depend upon the complexity of technological development; some of the most elaborate ritual patterns can be found in the simplest material cultures. The early Australian aborigines, with only a meager technological development, had a rich ritual life. Their rituals were, according to W. E. H. Stanner, evidence of the two abilities that have largely made human history what it is:

The first of these we might call "the metaphysical gift." I mean ability to transcend oneself, to make acts of imagination so that one can stand "outside" or "away from" oneself, and turn the universe, oneself, and one's fellows into objects of contemplation. The second ability is a "drive" to try to "make sense" out of human experience and to find some "principle" in the whole human situation.[1]

These human abilities Stanner understands as the basic source of both ritual and sacred images.

Ritual action, the dramatization of a significant event, is a major means of social integration. At its most fundamental level, ritual is the enactment of myth.[2] In the past, religious and political myths gave the members of a community a sense of their origins and destiny. In our present technological society, churches and synagogues often provide this kind of attunement to communal principles. For those who genuinely participate, the rituals offer occasions for identity and renewal. Through song, dance, and storytelling, people identify with their society. They gain a greater understanding of the whole of which each is a part. Although the mythic and aesthetic forms of ritual differ from culture to culture, its function remains the same — to provide an immediate, direct sense of involvement with the sacred, confirming the world view, indeed the very being, of the participant.

Throughout this chapter two concepts of ritual will be used. The first presupposes that ritual is rooted in a propensity for order, rhythmic patterning, and play — a propensity not exclusively human but observable in other creatures as well. In *Homo Ludens*, Johan Huizinga has set forth the idea that the ritual act itself, or an important part of it, remains within the play category. And as he has observed, if one accepts the Platonic definition of play as a spiritual activity, there is nothing irreverent in applying it to the most solemn ritual occasions.[3] The theologian Hugo Rahner expressed a similar idea when he wrote of the "dance of the spirit" and of the "game of grace."[4] Thus ritual activity may range in scope from the religious rites in which people seek attunement with supernatural power to professional and amateur sports, which provide a communion of spectators and players.

The play and patterning motifs in ritual act as both stabilizing forces and means of introducing novelty and flexibility. On the one hand, ritual organizes, confirms, and conserves; it operates as a kind of adhesive, binding people to each other and to modes of living that have stood the test of time. On the other hand, the play of ritual opens up new ways of being and thinking. Ritual activity can incorporate revolutionary elements. Victor Turner has emphasized the antistructuralist elements that generate process and change in social groups.[5] Plays, songs, and ceremonies that were once in the secular area may in time be absorbed into sacred ritual. And the reverse is also true. Symbolic forms that were once a part of sacred ceremonies — drama in the medieval church, for example — spin off into secular culture and take on a life of their own.

The second concept of ritual presupposes a mystical or supernatural dimension. In the ritual play of traditional religion, persons seek communion with transcendent being; the myths that are enacted point to the beginning and the beyond. Through faith, the participants perceive dimensions of space, time, and destiny beyond finite experience — an "assurance of things hoped for and the conviction of things not seen."[6] Viewed in this way, ritual is concerned with the life of the soul, rather than with the play, knowledge, and kinship we experience in politics or sports. This view may, in fact, devalue those other rituals one participates in as citizen or fan. But it does not contradict the experience of ritual as the inexorable playing we share with other creatures. Instead, it extends ritual play to include a cosmic "game" whose measures and rhythms we perceive only dimly.

Elements of Traditional Ritual

The ritualistic power of television to bind people together can be illuminated by an analysis of some basic elements of ritual experience. Taken together, these fundamental elements form an interpretive structure that can be placed like a grid over particular kinds of television images. Using such an analysis we can identify analogous as well as contrasting elements in television communication.

The first element, and perhaps the most important for understanding ritual, is the active participation of individuals. If one is to experience its power as a form of social integration, one cannot be a detached observer. The participant must actually live the truth of the enacted myth. This action transcends time and space and has an aesthetic unity that one does not experience in ordinary everyday life. In other words, persons are actors in a ritual and their bodily gestures and motions affect others in the drama.

Another basic component of ritual experience is the space in which the action occurs. Ritual space is extraordinary, set apart from the ordinary spaces of daily life and specifically appropriate for particular events. Its sacredness does not depend upon architectural complexity. It may simply be ground that is designated as sacred, as, for example, in the rituals of the Australian aborigines. Or, it may be an intricately designed space like that of Chartres cathedral.

In some traditional religions, ritual space involves special boundaries within which the presence of supernatural being is manifested. In that case it must be a fitting place for the holy and must allow for interaction between the divine and the human, between supernatural powers and finite creatures. Not all rituals, however, involve the presence of transcendent being. At its basic human level, ritual space must be related to the participation of the group and the action that occurs. Essentially it is space that is specially ordered for communion and interaction among persons with a common faith and loyalty.

A third element is the time in which ritual action takes place. Like ritual space, it is extraordinary in quality, not the ho-hum clock time of our workday. The time of ritual with its beginning, middle, and end is a carefully structured, cohesive unit. In time as we know it, we can point to a beginning, our birth, and we anticipate, ultimately, an ending in death. The middle, in-between, time stretches between these two poles. At no point in life are we able to perceive the whole of our existence, for ordinary time binds us to the middle. While we may conclude certain stages in our life cycle or accomplish certain projects, we can only experience the flow of the process. Ritual, on the other hand, deals with origin and destiny, the beginning and the end. Ritual casts us into measures that are outside ordinary time. The flow of everyday existence — open-ended and unresolved — is suspended and the believer leaps timelessly into creation and timelessly into eternity.

Extraordinary space and extraordinary time provide the context for the substantive core of ritual — the enactment of an event that is crucial for the life of the community and the individuals within it. The significant event that is enacted in ritual space and time is different for each religious tradition. The nature of the event depends upon the myths and history of the community. For some groups the events took place in the lives of historical figures such as Jesus of Nazareth or Buddha. Other ritual events involve "explanations" of what might be considered basically inexplicable phenomena, such as our fundamental origin and destiny. Australian aborigines, for example, had rituals that enacted the creation activity of Bolong the Rainbow Serpent. Whether the events are derived from historical persons and events, myths, or a combination of both, the constant element in all ritual action is the confirmation of the group and of the individual in the group. The repeated enactment of such events assures the group's power to generate loyalty and faith. Ritual action offers full participation in a world view, not simply a set of concepts.

Just as the substance of ritual events differs with each tradition, so does the interpretation. For some groups, the enactment of these events may be a form for remembering. In other traditions, participation enables the believer to transcend the ordinary time boundaries and be a part of the original event. In Catholic ritual, "remembrance" has ontological overtones —

to recall in order to live through the event. Communicants believe that through the grace of the sacrament they participate in the death, resurrection, and continuing being of Jesus. Ritual, in this sense, does more than "explain" the world. It creates the world, providing a sanctuary in which life is intensified. But, however widely the ontological interpretations of ritual action differ, the effect of participation in the drama is similar: believers experience a renewal of faith that sustains them as they return to ordinary time-space and its uncertainties.

The general pattern of ritual action, which involves withdrawal from the ordinary world into the extraordinary space, time, and action of ritual, transforms the person. Ritual participation can renew a person's faith in a center of values and meaning and can confirm one's place in a larger symbolic order. These experiences of renewal and confirmation occur, however, only to the degree that one is totally immersed in the ritual and its myth. For a disinterested observer a ritual might seem interesting or aesthetically pleasing but it would produce little effect. Tourists watching Hopi Indian dancers might be familiar with the myth involved, but they could not embrace it. The Indians do not dance to explain drought, to depict myth, or to illustrate tour books. For the Hopi who are still living in the myth, the rite and the myth are correlative. They dance in order to put themselves into a cosmic rhythm and to make it rain.[7]

Nor do rituals produce converts. Their power is manifested in the return of the believer from the sanctuary of metaphorical, ordered motions to the world of real life, better able to cope with its ordinariness and unpredictability. In addition to perpetuating the symbol systems of a tradition, repetition of ritual acknowledges the irresolution and disorder of common human experience. Even more, Eliade suggests, in repeating ritual one is

> tirelessly conquering the World, organizing it, transforming the landscape of nature into a cultural milieu. . . . Though the myths, by presenting them-

selves as sacrosanct models, would seem to paralyze human initiative, actually they stimulate [men and women] to create . . .[8]

With its ordered cosmos of space and time, ritual, then, confirms and transforms the believing individual who, with renewed imagination, returns to see and shape the ordinary world in a new way.

Telecasting Traditional Rituals

At the conclusion of a very moving religious ritual, the inaugural mass of Pope John Paul II in October 1978, the pope pronounced blessings on all those present in St. Peter's Square. This was immediately followed by another blessing on all those present through the media of television and radio. Just how many millions of believers were thus blessed would be hard to determine, but the blessed were no longer confined to the time-space event in St. Peter's Square. Throughout the world believing Christians had tuned in and watched this solemn, ancient ritual performed by the new spiritual leader of the Roman Catholic world. In some sense, television viewers had been "present" and through that presence had received the pope's blessings.

In the first section of this chapter, physical participation was discussed as one of the definitive elements of ritual. Today television takes countless viewers into important time-space events throughout the world. Although persons are not physically present, there is now an unprecedented opportunity for public participation in rituals that were once accessible to only a limited number of people. What is the nature of this transformation of ritual? What are some of its consequences? One new element is the electronic "ritual image." These electronic images contrast sharply with the ways images are employed in traditional ritual. For one who is physically present at a traditional ritual, the only visible images are those of liturgical objects or architectural surroundings, such as mosaics, wall hangings, or sculpture. There are also those ineluctable images formed in the mind's eye as it registers the setting, gestures, and movements of persons taking part in the ritual. The extraordinary dimension television has introduced is the continous sequence of images that links the viewer to ritual action occurring in a different part of the world. The ordered time and space of traditional rituals can become "present" for persons wherever time zones and spaces are penetrated by the technology of television. Radio, of course, first broke down some of the time-space barriers and initiated wide participation in public events. But the visual image has had more dramatic and far-reaching consequences. Its impact has been great largely because there is so much to be seen — dance, gesture, color, and movement in space. The inaugural mass of Pope John Paul II included vestments, liturgical objects, and the gestures and motions of human figures.

Through television, millions of viewers attended the Inaugural Mass of John Paul II

The ritual image on television also communicates aspects of visual splendor that eludes those who are physically present. Those attending a ritual generally have a limited mobility and thus a limited view of the action. In contrast, the television participant is extravagantly mobile. Depending upon the importance of the event, numbers of cameras provide multiple perspectives — breathtaking shots of architectural spaces and environmental panoramas, close-ups of objects and celebrants, studies of an action from two or three different angles. Think of the view of the inaugural mass presented. Where in St. Peter's Square could one have seen the architectural intricacies of the cathedral dome and the detailed liturgical gestures and expressions of Pope John Paul II? If one participates in certain rituals only through the televised images, these unreal perspectives and details add to the sense of involvement. But there is, to be sure, a falsification of experience in the unreal images of television, and it could be argued that this lavish, imagistic emphasis calls attention to unimportant details. Television viewers, for example, saw the modern wristwatch of the pope and heard a newscaster comment on it. This observation broke into the spirit and rhythm of the ritual and reminded viewers of the two different environments — one in St. Peter's Square and another shaped by the TV image. Although gaining a proxy participation through technology, viewers lost the immediacy of the sights, smells, and perspectives of large crowds.

With the accessibility to ritual space through television, two levels of participation have merged. Those who are physically present at the sacred site are joined by the committed, faithful watchers of the TV image. The real division, then, comes between the believer and the nonbeliever. The believer is one who does not budge from the TV set during the high points of the time-space event. The nonbeliever, on the other hand, does not even bother to turn it on. Occasionally, when different rituals compete for the same time period, stations must choose between them. When one network started the telecast of a professional football game twenty minutes late in order to cover the funeral of Pope John Paul I, telephone lines were jammed by angry football fans, upset over the disruption of their sacred time.

Americans mourned Hubert Humphrey's death as they watched honor guards carry his body down the steps of the Capitol

The communicative possibilities of ritual images and their capacity to accommodate large public participation have also made television increasingly important in American political experience. One intense and powerful example of this was the funeral of John F. Kennedy. A shocked, grieving public was given the opportunity to take part in the process of mourning. The televised images had a sacramental and healing quality that helped absorb the loss. Like participants in a ritual, persons watching found comfort in the "presence" of others who shared their sorrow. A similar extension of ritual experience occurred in the telecast of funeral services for Hubert H. Humphrey. Although the tone of these services differed, the role played by the ritual images was similar: They provided the public with the opportunity to share with family, friends, and political figures the funeral rites and sacrament. Those in the larger American family who felt they had lost an honored, beloved friend and who wished to assemble in his memory could do so. Those who wanted to be a part of the liturgical events were able, through the ritual image, to enter many spaces: the spaces and ceremonies of the Rotunda at the Capitol, the liturgical space of the church in Minnesota, and finally, the grave site where only a small number of people could physically come together. Millions heard the bugle sound taps and the honor guard fire the final salute in the January twilight. That ritual occasion was perhaps trivialized by the environments in which the telecast was received — a bar, the living room with the kids fighting, the kitchen where dinner was being prepared. Those who really cared about Senator Humphrey were there, and yet were not there. They saw the image, not the reality, of the ritual. But it was, nevertheless, a consolation.

The integrative and healing processes experienced by the American public when it mourns the deaths of its political leaders are instances of traditional rituals extended and transformed by television. Another example from political life is the inauguration of the president of the United States. This special event has generally been attended by a limited number of people. Now millions can take part through television. The telecast of Kennedy's inauguration taught us almost as much about the ritual power of television as did the images of his funeral. The inauguration, especially his speech, seemed to signal a new political awareness; citizens out there in electronic ritual space could join in this event. Political ritual has not been the same since.

Today, with the entrance of each new president, television coverage of the event and, even more important, the deliberate planning for such coverage, are increasingly elaborate. The inauguration is an institutionalized event which gives formal, symbolic authority to the most important leader in the American political system. Although it is a relatively short ceremony for such an authorization of power, an increasing amount of time has been given to programs and news relating to it. The telecasting of related events has created an elaborate pattern in which the inauguration itself is embedded.

In 1977, this enlarged ambiance included reports on the trainload of Jimmy Carter's followers departing for the inaugural events. Viewers who saw the president-elect wave them off in Plains, Georgia, also saw him greet them on their arrival in Washington. The "preinaugural gala" the evening before the big day was a giant variety show, commercially sponsored, where viewers glimpsed their favorite film and television stars. From time to time the cameras took viewers to the presidential box to see the president-elect and his family enjoying the festivities.

The following morning, Inauguration Day, the mood shifted from the carnival, celebrative atmosphere of the evening before to the sobriety of a morning prayer service. Telecast live from the Lincoln Memorial, the service was opened by Carter's pastor from Plains. But the dominant symbolic figure at the service was Martin Luther King, Sr. He provided the occasion for pictures of the late Martin Luther King, Jr., to be flashed upon the screen. In this particular mix — live coverage of the father and taped images of his slain son — television achieved dramatic visual effects especially designed for an audience watching at home.

After the prayer service, viewers were whisked away to the White House where the most important persons were gathering for morning coffee. The comings and goings of these political celebrities were photographed for fans to see. It was not long before the motorcade to the inaugural site began, and soon TV viewers were there, watching who was sitting next to whom in the specially designed seats — Billy, Miss Lillian, Amy. The ceremony itself, although relatively short, had strength and simple splendor. Carefully chosen music accompanied the major participants as they made their entrances. In contrast to the brisk rhythms of these processionals, the music used for Carter's entrance was slow and majestic. It was, in fact, the hymn that had been played when Kennedy's body was carried by the honor guard down the steps of the Capitol. Then came the major parts of the inauguration — the oath of office and the inaugural address. Several hours of television coverage led up to this important national event and hours more were to come.

Once the inauguration was over, Carter added his own aesthetic touch to the postinaugural festivities. As the motorcade drove away from the inaugural site, he and Mrs. Carter got out of the car — in what seemed to be a spontaneous gesture — and began walking down Pennsylvania Avenue. Soon after, they were joined by members of their family. Television viewers saw their new president doing something no other president had done — turn an ordinary motorcade into a jubilant recessional. There was some speculation that, far from being spontaneous, this act had been planned weeks in advance. If so, it only confirms the ritualistic intent, since most rituals are indeed carefully planned and staged.

For many viewers the continuous coverage of the inauguration events was boring. People who opposed Carter must have been indifferent to his inauguration. It is also possible that the steady viewers of game shows and soap operas saw this telecast ritual as an interruption of their daily fare. Feminists may have objected to watching a male-dominated ceremony. But for others, it meant visual participation in powerful and moving events. Although it obviously embroiders an important occasion, such coverage also reflects a sensitivity to the inauguration's significance as a ritualistic event. One of the critical elements in ritual activity is the believing, committed attitude of the persons taking part. Citizens with a strong loyalty to a party or political figure become, through the inauguration telecast, participants in a sacred event.

Secular Ritual

In our basically Protestant tradition there is generally less expressed concern for liturgical rhythms and rituals than in a Catholic culture. If symbolizing is fundamental to human existence and if ritual is one way of accomplishing that, then, even in a Protestant environment, rituals arise outside of traditional institutions. Secular society, in fact, frequently develops its own sacramental forms.

One of the most obvious and popular examples of secular ritual is professional sports, especially football. A sports announcer once described the telecast event as a "tiny sanctuary in real life" — a description that could be a popular one-line definition of ritual. The Super Bowl represents the ultimate in ritualization. It has become a sacramental occasion more familiar, even to those who are not fans, than many events in the Christian liturgical year. Super-Sunday for most Americans refers not to Pentecost or the beginning of Advent but to Super Bowl Sunday. The big day is heralded in all the media and is generally featured on the cover of *TV Guide*. As with the inauguration of a president, there are pregame programs beginning the night before and others starting early Sunday morning. Some parts of the half-time entertainment specials are designed primarily for the television audience. In the shows that follow the game, superstars from the sports and entertainment world are featured.

Less obvious than the ritualization of sports is the ritualization of various political processes and of the nightly news programs. Like professional football and traditional rituals, political conventions, election coverage, and the nightly news are reshaped by television.

Looking first at political conventions, there is probably no way of knowing all that is going on at the different levels of human interaction — no way, really, to "cover" conventions like these. As television reporting has increased over the last twenty years, however, viewers have begun to have a sense of what is going on. The constant, complicated camera work brings viewers into the political realities. Live telecasts of the conventions, even to casual TV viewers, produce some degree of political awareness. Certainly, actions that are not accessible to the omnipresent camera continue to take place; the delegates are involved in unreported kinds of political activities. But TV coverage of the conventions has opened up new opportunities for public participation. Millions of viewers all over the nation become present through the electronic image.

Walter Cronkite anchoring CBS news coverage of the 1980 Republican Convention in Detroit, Michigan

The convention lends itself to ritualization because its very structure contains ritual elements. The event takes place in extraordinary space and has special time boundaries, running four days with formal opening and closing ceremonies. The space is perhaps more dramatically presented to the TV viewers than to those physically present. It is frequently described by commentators as the cameras sweep over the interior. Viewers are moved from one place to another — the podium, the floor of the auditorium, the galleries. Most intriguing is the press box, where commentators sit like high priests. Some of the political personalities are interviewed in this special space.

The ritualization of the central event — the selection of the presidential and vice-presidential candidates — varies from convention to convention. Sometimes the event actually resembles the Super Bowl, where there are real struggles between competing quarterbacks, and fans are howling and blowing horns in the stands. At other times, especially when the primaries have more or less determined the outcome, the selection resembles a liturgical event. Although there may appear to be some kind of struggle between the god of light and the god of darkness, certain knowledge of the outcome gives more opportunity for luxurious ritual play.

In 1976, the Republican convention resembled the Super Bowl. The television commentators even called attention to the "battle of the wives," as Mrs. Ford cheered her team in one part of the "stadium" and Mrs. Reagan led cheers for the other team. Disruptions from the floor during the drama of the selection became a standard feature of this convention. Even on the last evening when Ford was chosen as the candidate, Reagan supporters continued their devotion to him. In the closing moments when all participants — those at the convention and those at home — expected a glowing reconciliation at the podium, the crowd still registered disharmony. Reagan supporters were not easy losers.

Perhaps because Carter — through his victories in the primaries — had virtually won the nomination before the 1976 convention, the Democrats, intentionally or unintentionally, exploited the ritualistic possibilities of the event. A rich variety of personages embellished the liturgical drama. Political heroes and heroines were highlighted in various parts of the program. It was Barbara Jordan, a black woman and a very powerful speaker, who sparked the first night. There was no way to measure the effect of her presence, but she was an inspiring figure for women all over the country. During the next four days of the convention there was a political model for everyone, liberal or conservative: Cesar Chavez, Yvonne B. Burke, Jerry Brown, Hubert Humphrey, George Wallace. Even the draft resisters were represented. On one touching occasion when the paralyzed Vietnam veteran, Kovac, nominated one of the resisters for the vice-presidency, the two embraced at the podium. It was later reported that the event was staged, but as with Carter's walk down Pennsylvania Avenue, that simply reinforced the ritualistic intent.

Another unusual aspect of the convention was the simultaneous telecasting of images. As various speakers came and went, cameras on the floor picked up audience reactions as well as the image of the speaker. When the delegates were casting their votes, images from the convention floor were mixed with live shots from Carter's hotel room. Viewers saw Carter sitting with his mother, daughter, and grandson, watching the proceedings of the convention floor on their TV set. Then, at the very moment of victory, when there was a sufficient number of votes to assure him the candidacy, two live images were blended. Through the wizardry of technology, viewers saw the image of the victorious Carter in his hotel room simultaneously with the image of Mrs. Carter on the convention floor surrounded by reporters. What viewers saw was Carter watching himself watch himself. Carter must have had supreme confidence to permit this kind of symbolic telecast.

The final video spectacular of the 1976 Democratic convention came after the last speech. The Reverend Martin Luther King, Sr., gave the benediction. On their TV sets, viewers saw his expressive face and heard the Southern black preacher communicate with the Almighty, invoking blessings for the group. Viewers also saw, through a shift of cameras, Carter's face, hand on his chin, as he echoed a soft "Amen" to the prayer. Then came the parade of heroes and heroines, filing up to the podium in a great collection of video portraiture: Jerry Brown, Hubert Humphrey, Coretta King, George Wallace. Everyone moved about on the podium in a harmonious waltz. All joined in singing "We Shall Overcome."

Commercials, paid for by corporations, brought the convention rituals into the homes of the American public. While the conventions offered cross-sections of political opinions, the commercials indexed viewers' production and consumption: automobiles, dog food, underwear, soaps. Some commercials were the same for both conventions. On CBS, for example, Playtex and Volkswagen were among the sponsors for both the Democrats and the Republicans.

In November 1976, after a densely packed autumn of televised debates, political commercials, and opinion polls, election night came. Each of the three national networks prepared its own environment and format: charts, specially colored lights and maps, computers. Complex connections had been established in different sections of the country so that commentators could bring in live coverage from strategic places. The commercial advertisers were lined up and ready to hawk their wares. Cameras and newsmen took their positions at campaign headquarters and in spaces designated for victory celebrations. The viewer who cared about pictures and politics would soon be saturated with blinking lights; red, white, and blue maps of the United States; percentages and polls. Once a substantial number of precincts reported their results, the predictions, tabulations, and projections would begin flashing onto the viewers' screens.

While election night may not conform as closely to ritual structure as does the political convention, still it contains a number of ritualistic elements. The networks have appropriated and ritualized election night as a sports event. While it provides information and entertainment, it also draws millions of Americans together into an impassioned mass.

The candidates and their families are often well positioned on election night. As the computers projected Carter's victory in 1976, ABC immediately sent out images of Miss Lillian down in Georgia. At the moment of victory, Miss Lillian stood up, threw open her coat and revealed a JIMMY WON T-shirt.

Behind her, in similar gestures a mini–chorus line of Carter supporters exposed their JIMMY WON T-shirts as well. Later on, viewers saw Jimmy and Rosalynn return to Plains to greet friends. One of the last images telecast in the early-morning hours was Carter carrying a sleeping Amy into their home.

The election night ritual is not over until the loser formally concedes the victory. The morning after the 1976 election Gerald Ford's statement was read with grace and dignity by Mrs. Ford on behalf of her husband, who was too hoarse to speak. Election night was over. There would be no such ritual for another four years. Yet those viewers who happened to see the reporting of the off-year elections in 1978 could see new ritual environments being tested. Innovative lights, new bright maps and charts, and computers were being put in readiness for Campaign 1980.

In 1980 TV viewers saw some unusual ritualistic elements at the Republican convention. The dramatic action centering around the choice of Ronald Reagan's vice-presidential running mate brought rumors and speculations, minute by minute, to those who tuned in. On the third evening of the convention, Walter Cronkite interviewed vice-presidential hopeful Gerald Ford and his wife, Betty. This interview allowed viewers to witness an unprecedented deliberation; apparently Ford was still weighing the pros and cons of joining the Reagan ticket as a "co-president." Some commentators later speculated that through the interview Ford was continuing his conversations with Reagan, as well as addressing the television public. Rumors about a Reagan-Ford ticket intensified during the evening, and there was widespread feeling that a deal had been struck between the two men. Meanwhile, George Bush, a discouraged aspirant, was reported to have conceded, "It looks like it's all set . . ." Evidently resigned to the alleged Reagan-Ford ticket, Bush cut his convention speech short by several minutes.

Excitement mounted during the roll call, and, as expected, Reagan was acclaimed the victorious candidate. Simultaneously, images were telecast live from the convention floor and from Reagan's hotel suite. The happy victor and his family saw their images and those from the convention blended on the TV screen. In the midst of the joyous demonstrations, however, all the networks busily forwarded hints to viewers that the deal between Ford and Reagan was off. They reported that George Bush had, in fact, received a call from Ronald Reagan inviting him to be his running mate. Even more excitement was generated when Reagan broke with tradition and came directly to the arena to address the delegates and announce his choice.

On the fourth and last evening of the convention, the Republicans' sense of togetherness resounded throughout all the activities. Prime time was saturated with happiness and harmony. When festivities formally ended, loyal Republicans turned off their television sets, renewed and ready for battle.

The convention styles of 1976 were reversed for the two major parties in 1980. The Republican convention was a ritualistic confirmation of Reagan's candidacy similar to the one Jimmy Carter had received from his party four years earlier. Conversely, the Democratic convention had to cope with and conceal divided loyalties within the party, as the Republicans had in 1976. But, whatever the differences in convention styles, both Reagan and Carter had their campaigns ceremoniously launched in prime-time public view. John Anderson, the independent challenger, had no such symbolic time, space, or ritualistic form to dramatize and confirm his candidacy.

In the fall of 1980 TV viewers followed the major candidates through campaign speeches, polls and eventually two debates. The debates themselves spawned still more polls and debates about winners and losers. Finally came November 4. Voters made their choices during the day and in the evening tuned in to follow the dramatic interaction of computers, blinking lights, colored maps and commentators. *TV Guide* provided advice to viewers watching the events, indexing the times at which voting results might be expected. Before 10:00 P.M., commentators and President Carter alike agreed: Ronald Reagan had won the election. American voters had switched political channels and were prepared to tune in to the actor/politician who projected a soothing and trustworthy presence on television. Interested and enthusiastic Reagan supporters could look forward to the ritual of his inauguration and the preinaugural extravaganzas of January 1981.

The Super Bowl and World Series come only once a year and national conventions and election nights come once in four. But the public receives steady, if less spectacular, ritualistic nourishment through regularly broadcast professional sports such as football, baseball, basketball, and hockey. And every evening, without fail, there is the nightly news.

It will be remembered that ancient ritual provided its participants with an explanation of what the world was like; myths enacted in rituals explained the world to the believer. One difficulty in using myth to interpret newscasts is the common misunderstanding of the term. *Myth* is frequently interpreted as "falsehood" or "fantasy." Persons forget that myths enacted in ritual were ways of knowing and mediating truths about reality. It is this orienting and explanatory quality of myth that is found in the nightly news. The news presents public symbols through which contemporary persons understand reality.

The ritualistic power of the nightly news is due, in part, to its regularly scheduled time and uniform presentation. At a precise hour every evening viewers tune in their favorite national news program to find out what is going on. They read newspapers at random times and places, but the presentation of the nightly news is a shared perception of order and events. This collective viewing provides community solidarity since countless citizens are exposed to identical explanations of current realities.

Within the format of the nightly newscast there are patterns within patterns. Units within the half-hour segment are carefully organized in order of importance. Through words and pictures viewers get a sense of what is "true" — what is going on in the nation, Europe, Asia, even the cosmos. Outside of their immediate worlds of family and neighborhood, the nightly news tells viewers how it is, how things came to be, what might be expected.

Intermingled at regular intervals with information about national, international, and cosmic events are the sponsors' advertisements. Although detested by many, the commercials — in addition to making the program possible — play a comforting role. Many of the "truths" of the news deal with national and world events that are often dismal, tragic, without easy solution or resolution. The commercials break that mood of irresolution. One can, in fact, be comforted that there are some problems that are simple enough to be resolved through deodorants, laxatives, denture creams, cereals, antihistamines, or motor oil. The commercials set limits to the accounts of hard news and irreconcilable issues. They bring comfort where there might otherwise be none.

Taken together, the alternating news and commercials give us a tightly packaged symbolic record of reality. When Walter Cronkite said ". . . and that's the way it is. . .," many people had confidence in that knowledge. Viewers may know that the news gives incomplete, often misleading, information; still, to many, the camera does not lie. Ritualized by television, the symbols become the "reality."

According to sociologist Herbert J. Gans, journalists perform an important function when they report the actions and statements of national figures. In so doing, they help to form our concepts of the nation and of society. Moreover, through print and electronic media they are constantly reminding us of the reality and power of these human constructs — "nation" and "society." While journalists enhance the position of national leaders through their reporting, they also "inform an audience which lives in micro-societies that are often far removed from nation and society." Gans comments:

Whether or not the audience actually needs information about them is a crucial question I cannot answer. Suffice it to say that news supplies that information. But when people say they keep up with the news, they may also be saying that they are maintaining contact with nation and society.[9]

One of the journalists' major functions is, in Gans's opinion, to manage, with others, the "symbolic arena" or public stage for communication. Because many people try to get their messages in and keep other messages out, the symbolic arena is a political battleground, and the management of it is a major political issue.

In many countries, the issue is foreclosed because the government in power is its manager; in other countries, news organizations and journalists manage the arena, with the government retaining veto power. In America, the news firms are the nominal managers, but news organizations and journalists are the actual ones. In the process, they also regulate individuals and groups with messages; and, in so doing, they maintain order in the symbolic arena.[10]

Electronic Politics

Traditional rituals maintain social systems, but they can also change the systems. Roland A. Delattre, a scholar in American studies, writes of the creative role that ritual plays in our capacity to reorder as well as conserve: "Rituals may celebrate and confirm the rhythms and shape of an established version of reality, but they may also celebrate and render articulate the shape and rhythms of a new emergent version."[11]

Today the ritualistic patterning of television is changing the ways in which we think about and participate in our political processes. TV coverage of the 1976 and 1980 presidential campaigns emphasized activities which, before television, received little national attention. Extensive reporting of debates, caucuses, and primaries has increased the gamelike elements in politics. The events receive special attention and the rhythms of the primary campaigns have become a regular feature of the nightly news. Whereas the caucus was at one time a provincial affair in which decisions were made on the basis of direct contact between local politicians and workers, it is now a momentous media event that can enhance or detract from the aspiring candidates. Caucuses and primaries are like the Super Bowl playoffs. In fact, some of the terminology of professional sports has moved into the political sphere. Tuesday, June 3, 1980, became Super Tuesday because of the large number of primaries being held on that day and the unusually large number of delegates at stake in those contests.

Television news allows viewers to see and hear candidates in a unique kind of political portraiture. The candidates' images are like those of football heroes who are dramatically making end runs or successfully completing long passes. TV cameras, of course, also record the fumbles. The filmed replays of heroic actions or fumbles can circulate for days on local stations and national networks. John Anderson's statement favoring gun registration before a New Hampshire audience adamantly opposed to controls brought TV viewers the image of a candidate with guts.

Television news also packages dramatic action during political campaigns. Each evening viewers take their places at their sets and "live" in these dramatizations. As a result, this daily ritualization of the state primaries has shifted the process for selecting candidates from the national conventions to the earlier contests. On the basis of his commanding victories in the primaries, it was clear by early June 1980 that Ronald Reagan had enough delegates to win the candidacy of the Republican party. The convention was for him, as it was for Carter in 1976, a ritualistic celebration.

The changes in the quality and pace of political campaigning have been interpreted in various ways by participants and analysts. Jerry Brown, a presidential hopeful in 1980, said that the political process has been reduced to a chapter in *Wide World of Sports*. Political analyst Kevin Phillips, a participant on *The MacNeil/Lehrer Report*, following the Massachusetts and Vermont primaries, spoke of the "volatile" nature of the campaign:

PHILLIPS: Well, maybe it's just a cliché. . .I suspect

that the people are sufficiently disillusioned; they're
not 100% sure what they are looking for; they're not
sure what these politicians are; they go by on a
screen. People don't know anything about a George
Bush until all of a sudden, presto, George Bush wins.
Then you start finding out what George Bush *is*, and
maybe you don't like it. So you shift away from him,
and then John Anderson flashes up there with his
31% and he's the hype. I think it's a very unfortunate thing. I think it's not the media's fault, it's the
fault of a system, the interaction of the media, the
fragmentation of the political process, the long
drawn-out thing but — sure, it's volatile. It's also
a mess.[12]

Yet Jim Lehrer, co-host of *The MacNeil/Lehrer Report*, pointed
out that people were turning out in record numbers to vote.
Another guest, Robert Shogan of the Los Angeles *Times*,
responded:

SHOGAN: Well, yeah, that's what *is* interesting. I
don't know. Maybe it's a second stage. Not long ago,
people were just staying home in record numbers and
publishers were commissioning books about voter
apathy, and now we've got this voter restiveness that
the darned people won't stay home where they
belong. They're turning out, the independents are
voting, and it's upsetting everybody's prediction.[13]

Martin Linsky, media consultant to the Ford Foundation
and the Institute of Politics at Harvard University, has voiced a
positive attitude toward media-effected changes in the elec-
toral process. In "The System's Working Just Fine," an article in
the Boston *Globe*, he said that we were engaged in a "great experiment." The emphasis of the media upon the primaries is
"democratizing the process," taking the power to pick the
presidential nominees away from party bosses and special
interest groups and entrusting it to voters. "We are trusting
their good judgment and the capacity of the nation's news

media for keeping them informed." While there are "kinks" in the system, the surveys have shown a high degree of awareness of the candidates and their stands on issues. Rather than damage the system, the representation of events on television contributes positively to it; candidates themselves must respond to the changes.

> Television is the fastest, most intense, universal medium of communication devised so far. Every aspirant to national leadership in contemporary America must have among his or her skills the ability to communicate well on the tube and a finely tuned sense that the presence of television has shortened the time available for decision making.[14]

Politics and politicians are "caught up in a wider and genuine revolution, which is affecting almost every aspect of society," wrote Philip L. Geyelin, editor of the editorial page of the *Washington Post*. TV is part of a technological revolution in the field of communications and in computers as they relate to canvassing, polling, phone banks, and mail campaigns. He spoke of the changes in political events, such as a political rally, which is "staged almost entirely for the purpose of attracting television attention and getting the candidate on the evening news, where millions, as distinct from hundreds," can see and hear. He quoted the observations of Douglass Cater, analyst of politics and communications, who wrote in the London *Sunday Times*:

> After a quarter of a century's phenomenal growth, television has created a communication environment in no way comparable to the world of books, plays, cinema, newspapers and periodicals. Its ceaseless flow of electronic signals . . . affects fundamentally not merely our thoughts but the way we go about the business of thinking collectively. Society swims in this environment and is hardly conscious of its consequences.[15]

Geyelin concludes that this revolution is not all for the bad, but certainly not all for the good. It does threaten "a massive overloading of the thought processes which could blow out the political system unless we can adjust to it."

Whether viewed positively or negatively, the ritualized news patterns that flow across the screen each evening have contributed substantively to changing our political processes and to shaping our common electronic environment. Moreover, the format of the nightly news, along with other media, has nurtured persistent criticism of government action and of politicians in power.

In this chapter ritual has been used to interpret certain kinds of television communication; in the next chapter traditional icons, or sacred images, will help us understand some of the other ways that television communicates world views and standards of human behavior.

II
Icon: From Sacred Symbol to Video Myth

Wherever we encounter images — on billboards and posters in the street, through television screens, or in museums — we are seeing small segments of human experience made visible. The imagemaker has turned a selected bit of experience into an "object of contemplation." Whether moving frames or static marks on paper, all images are products of this fundamental symbolizing ability.

The icon is a special example of a symbolic form that is used for the objectification of beliefs and for self-transcendence. Though it may be meaningful for certain individuals, an icon is not generated by self-expression. It may manifest an aesthetic complexity and richness, but it is not motivated primarily by an aesthetic impulse. Its roots are in the Greek word *eikon*, or "image," and in general usage it simply means pictorial representation. However, *icon* also refers to an important kind of image, one that is intended to bring persons into relation with the sacred through visual narration of sacred stories or portrayal of sacred personages.[1] In this sense, icon is comparable to ritual in integrating individuals into a social whole. In the same manner in which ritual has been used, icon can serve as an analogue to help in understanding some of the ways in which contemporary belief systems and values are communicated through television.

Traditional Icons

Like ritual, icon has been borrowed from more compact and unified societies. First, we need to consider how the traditional icon communicated a society's faith.

Icons as Symbolization of Order

Traditional religious icons in Western and Eastern Christianity gave people a basic orientation to human experience. Sacred icons presented the faithful beholder with a concrete, meaningful world. Whether they portrayed a sacred past or anticipated a sacred future, icons provided a sense of origin, destiny, and participation in that order. In the midst of elusive, capricious, and uncertain happenings, people could relate to a larger chain of events transcending private and particular moments in time. Icons could assuage the sense of isolation and meaninglessness. Even though the sacred events represented might be outside the observer's immediate, transitory world, icons furnished contexts in which the faithful could locate their own present experiences. Icons were visual explanations of a larger symbolic order of time and space that helped to make sense of the ordinary world.

Icons as Models of Human Behavior

For those believers who paid serious attention, human figures depicted in the sacred narratives provided examples to be admired and imitated. The notion that someone was able to cope or deal with life in an extraordinary and exemplary way brought inspiration and comfort to a bored and disillusioned existence. In the traditional icons, whether they were sacred personages mediating grace or humble persons receiving new life, the luminous figures held out a special kind of hope to or-

dinary persons. Saints and heroes took on power as representa-
tive figures that, at the least, offered less privileged human
beings a vicarious experience of adventure, of risk, and endurance of suffering. Paradoxically, saintliness symbolized gaining one's life while losing it in a greater cause.

Icons as Boundaries of Questions and Answers

At the same time that the traditional sacred icon located
the individual in a world that transcended the present one, it
evoked what some people today might consider irrelevant
questions about eternal life, salvation, action toward one's
neighbor, and justice. Whatever comfort the beholder might receive regarding origin or end, there were burdensome problems
for the life between. Thus icons were often moralistic and persuasive, a kind of visual catechism. Individuals could learn to
cope with moral problems by reflecting on the sacred images,
by experiencing their presence or by contemplating the mythic
actions represented. While icons were not, of course, the only
means for communication about human action, in premodern
societies they played an informative, perhaps awesome, role in
articulating virtues and vices, rewards and punishments. For
instance, the marvelous sculptures in the Romanesque church
at Vézelay, France, were so powerful that Bernard of Clairvaux
feared the monks would study them rather than their books.

Yet the range of questions raised by the icons was not
limitless. In visually depicting moral issues, the icons set
boundaries as well. One could, in fact, make up some very interesting profiles of cultures on the basis of the questions that
were put forth and resolved. In early Christian and medieval
churches, icons presented questions and answers that put human action and events in a framework both inside and outside
history. Pictures of the disciples' activities directed the viewer's attention to questions of faith, service to one's neighbor,
and loyalty to Christ. In the imagery of contemporary culture
we are more accustomed to the questions and answers posed
by advertisers. These images direct us to achieving success,

owning a great range of products, and becoming beautiful, healthy people in the here and now.

Illustrative of the three roles that traditional icons played in premodern society are mosaics in the church of San Apollinare Nuovo in Ravenna, Italy. One of these, *Christ Healing the Paralytic*, provides a visual metaphor for what is essentially an invisible order of being — the Lordship of Christ. Through sustained attention to such an icon the believer can "know" the unknowable whole and feel a part of that symbolic order. The same image offers models for human action: the believer who is healed, the disciple, and Christ himself. This image and others in the series of mosaics frame the questions and resolutions set forth in the ministry and Passion of Christ. Where there is belief and confidence in the symbolic whole, epistemology and ontology are intertwined. The image enables viewers both to perceive and to participate in that larger order which transcends their particular existence.

American Icons

In most religions icons are derived from sacred scripture and legends. Early Protestantism, however, had a strong bias against images in churches and provided no context for them and no patronage for the artist. The dominant forms through which meanings were communicated were verbal and musical. Ritual actions were simplified and the architectural spaces for worship had no sacramental images. Nor was there a general public space appropriate for pictures with traditional religious subjects. In view of the biases against sacred images that have filtered through American cultural history and the lack of popularity of such images with the general public, how can one speak of American icons?

A key to understanding American icons is to remember the function of the icon — to articulate and shape beliefs through visual forms. This role can be performed by secular as well as by religious images. This is especially true in American culture. Indeed, to the degree that traditional religious institutions in this culture have emphasized the "word" and de-emphasized images, they have deprived themselves of the power of images to transmit their own symbols. And, it may be that, ironically, the sacramental power of images in American society has been most effectively taken over by television.

Today, just as in the past, persons use images to locate themselves in a larger frame of reference. The fact that contemporary American culture is highly pluralistic does not mean that public symbols are unimportant. The multiplicity of relative "truths" in American society may actually enhance the capability of television images to provide common myths. Even though the symbolic constructs and values may be shallow, the very pervasiveness of the medium provides a means to connect many of the differentiated and disconnected segments of our lives.

While most imagemakers in this country have paid scarce attention to traditional sacred images, both "high" and "popular" artists have persistently used certain metaphors in expressing and identifying common visions and sentiments. Without relying on the iconography of institutional religion, American artists have made use of three types of icons: *the common life* — family, neighborhood, city, nation; *nature*; and *technology*. These public symbols, deeply rooted in this culture, have become the source for the iconography on television. As TV critic Horace Newcomb has observed, ". . . we must recognize that the ideas and the symbols that express them on television are not 'created' there. They have a history in American culture. They are 'used' ideas and symbols. . ."[2] The three visual metaphors identified have been present in American art from the beginning and were appropriated by artists as they expressed and shaped public loyalties.

Family

The most basic and at the same time the most complex orders are those linking us as human beings, one to another, and the one to the many: family, neighborhood, working community, state, and nation. Each of these communities has its own principles of organization, its own convictions and myths. Large communities — the nation, for example — are most easily represented by a conventional symbol such as the United States flag. In the working community, certain groups are designated by symbols derived from their characteristic attire — hard hats or blue collars.

One of the most persistent ways of representing communities and their myths involves the narrative use, the storytelling possibilities, of the human figure. Images of human interaction — people in relation to each other, the gestures, expressions, and visual language of the human body — depict significant events in the history and myths of a particular group. Throughout cultural history, in painting and sculpture, representations of the human figure have embodied and communicated societal values. Today that tradition is continued through photography, film, and, particularly, television.

As our memberships in groups frequently overlap and intertwine, so do the images representing these groups. Perhaps because of its power to articulate myths and values that extend beyond its immediate scope, the image of the family has been frequently used as a metaphor for larger communities. No matter what sociological factors in family life are revealed through statistical studies, it takes only a casual glance at television offerings to see how often the family is used to show a "world" within which questions of human behavior are set forth.

The family has been a major metaphorical image throughout American cultural history. In the early years of this nation, when there was little institutional support for the visual arts, the portrait painter was in demand at nearly all levels of society. Family portraits, seen today in museums, provide a rich mosaic of concepts of American family life. One sees personal possessions, furniture, glimpses of the environment, expressions and gestures of family members. All of these elements witness to those visible entities and invisible values that, taken together, give the modern viewer a concrete sense of what was considered of worth. From the long tradition of family portraits to the instamatic images and replay movies, the family portrait — still or in motion — is a private icon that most Americans hold dear.

From the nineteenth century, Currier and Ives prints offer a rich portrayal of the accepted ideas about the family. Some of them show changing roles and processes in family life. Others show the family in its physical environment — the family in a rural setting, moving westward, or settling on the frontier. The representational elements — mother and father, children, dress, gestures, physical surroundings — are not to be seen primarily as evidence of what life was actually like, but as symbolic records.

The familiar images of Norman Rockwell's magazine covers and illustrations are similarly informative about the early twentieth century. They are concrete embodiments of life in a particular time-space moment. On the pages of magazines, Rockwell's images made his interpretations accessible to others for whom these images became ways of "seeing" their own experiences. Although Rockwell portrayed relationships within the nuclear family, his images also moved outward and symbolized the space of a small town: the corner drugstore, the barber shop, Main Street.

To be sure, Rockwell's visual reflections on small-town experiences often differed from those of other imagemakers. Norman Rockwell's families were unlike those of Farm Security Administration photographers such as Dorothea Lange and Ben Shahn. Documenting the plight of American migrant workers on the move in the 1930s, these photographers often showed family life as stark, desperate, dreary. Still, the family was a world in which both painters and photographers could place human figures and narrate visually the dramas, events, and experiences characteristic of life at that time. Thus, although the imaginative visual reflections differed from artist to artist, the metaphorical family image remained a constant reference for statements about the common life.

The family is unique in that it is a human community in

which the "oneness" or wholeness of the group and its parts can be perceived in a single setting. Although there are many invisible communities in which a person participates, it is the family that can be most convincingly made visible. The painter or photographer can identify the whole by its parts and can present the totality bounded by the frame of the picture. By contrast, other social orders — neighborhood, city, state, nation — must be represented visually by conventional symbols or general views that obscure the individual parts.

Moreover, the visualization of the family unit often has a social dimension. A Currier and Ives print depicting family life in the nineteenth century includes concepts not only of family life, but also of the environment and culture. The interior ornamentation of the home, together with its surroundings, connect the family unit with larger communities.

Small enough to allow for dramatic personal interaction, yet large enough to reflect social norms, the family has also been a consistent visual metaphor in television programming. Very early in television history the nuclear family became the subject of dramas, comedies, and soap operas, and it is equally pervasive today.[3] While portrayals of family life in early programs such as *Mama* and *Father Knows Best* are unlike representations in programs of the 1970s and 1980s such as *Eight Is Enough* or *One Day at a Time*, the metaphor has remained constant. The family provides a symbolic background that can be shaped to accommodate a great diversity of characters and moral principles.

At the same time, it is one of the most easily understood worlds with which viewers can identify. In contrast to nature or technology, the metaphor of the family depicts our closest, most intense interpersonal involvements. Through family relationships we know love, trust, respect, fidelity, nurture, the struggle for independence, and the routine give and take of everyday living. The family can also be the community in which we learn to cope with human suffering — loss of love, distrust, infidelity, or a breakdown of support and nurturing. Interpersonal relationships in the family are the source for the fundamental role models of mother, wife, father, husband, sister, and brother. In addition, family-centered images, especially those on television, communicate in a very direct way a variety of attitudes toward material possessions, social status, vocational concerns, and involvement with larger social and political orders.

Every TV family show — whether trite or profound — offers concerned viewers an opportunity to analyze the ways in which social norms are implicitly or explicitly present. But, since TV images have such a lifelike, intimate quality, one has to make a deliberate effort to see them primarily as symbolic records. Every series has a distinct visual environment that contributes to the portrayal of the family. In that environment, activities and concerns move the family members along from episode to episode. Each program, from the opening scenes to the final captions and credits, is a carefully structured sequence of images. Prominent TV families can be studied just like a Currier and Ives print or a Norman Rockwell cover.

The environment of the Bunkers in *All in the Family* was a working-class neighborhood, always seen in the introductory shots when the camera took the viewer on an auto ride past brown frame houses in Queens. The Bunkers' house was a small one, and much of the action in the show took place in the combined living and dining area, separated from the kitchen by a traditional swinging door. Decoration and furnishings helped to establish the taste and personalities of Edith and Archie Bunker. There was a large, ordinary stuffed chair (now in the Smithsonian) that was only for Archie. Parallel to this chair was Edith's, a somewhat smaller one, less suitable for lounging; it was offered to guests or strangers who came in. Both chairs faced the television set. The wallpaper was patterned, and light bulbs in the wall lamps were shaped like candle flames. Near the front door hung a reproduction of a seascape with a sailing ship; nearby stood a coat rack. Stairs from the living area led up to the second-floor bedrooms, comfortable but not elegant in their furnishings. There was only one bathroom for the household, and the noise of the flushing

toilet could be heard downstairs. The kitchen was Edith's do-
main and the family meals provided frequent opportunities for
interaction among the characters. Both the kitchen door and
the front door opened onto a neighborhood where persons
knew and visited with each other.

There were, of course, other environments. In the early
years of the series Archie was a dock foreman for the Prender-
gast Tool and Die Company. And there was Kelsey's Bar, which
Archie was later to purchase. Mike, the son-in-law, went
through college; Gloria had a job. All of the characters moved
in and out of a variety of places as characters and plot changed.
But the major action of the series generally rotated around the
Bunker home.

Although Archie's Place later became the primary locus of
action, most viewers will remember the front door of 704
Houser Street rattling and banging as Archie burst in, taking
off his old red and gray plaid jacket and well-worn hat, shouting all the time for Edith. From his armchair or at the kitchen
table, Archie would argue or engage in shouting matches with
other members of his family. Through these central characters
— Archie, Edith, their daughter, Gloria, and son-in-law, Mike
— and their interactions, many social issues and values of the
1970s were brought to life. Over the years themes of conflict,
prejudice, even violence, were introduced with a kind of vivid-
ness that had not appeared in prime-time situation comedy.
For many, the Bunkers represented "realism" in family and
social life. Actors Carroll O'Connor, Jean Stapleton, Sally
Struthers, and Rob Reiner transformed symbolic types into recognizable human beings.

Archie was the symbol of an uneducated, working-class,
prejudiced, middle-aged male, whose wisecracks about "spics,"
"spades," "chinks," "wops," and "kikes" delineated his character. Mike Stivic, whom Archie referred to as Meathead, was
a central character, representing the conflict of social attitudes
presented in the plots. Polish-American and politically liberal,
he was studying for his degree in sociology while he and Gloria
were living with Edith and Archie. Watching the series, one be-

came accustomed to the roles the characters played in expressing and defending particular positions — whether the Equal Rights Amendment or gun control legislation. For Archie "Ms." was a "near 'miss,'" and in one episode he went on the air against gun control. Yet, interspersed throughout the series were many dramatic episodes showing nuances of temperament and personality. Particularly poignant were the times when Archie was laid off from work. What he suffered and what befell him in this experience evoked the viewer's sympathy and sense of identification. But Archie's strength as a symbol depended upon the consistency with which he was portrayed as an opinionated, outspoken, prejudiced man. This fundamental aspect of his character was a catalytic force in the drama.

Edith and Archie Bunker from *All in the Family* have become popular secular icons

Edith Bunker rushed to and fro through the swinging door of the kitchen to greet Archie, fetch him a beer, or scurry around getting meals for the family. The ordinariness of her print dresses seemed to blend in with the wallpaper design and furniture. Visits to the beauty parlor were reserved for special occasions, such as the time she finally maneuvered Archie into taking a second honeymoon. Archie frequently referred to her as Ding-bat, as she had a roundabout, prolonged way of relating incidents. In spite of her twittery façade, she was the pivotal person in the household when it was time to think straight. While her symbolic role involved subservience to Archie, she represented, equally strongly, the values of honesty, tolerance, traditional religion, and faith. It was she who mediated differences between Mike and Archie and she who enjoyed friendship with the black family next door, the Jeffersons.

The camera work and acting contributed substantially to the authenticity of the major characters. Frequently the full frame of the TV screen was filled with the face of one of the principal actors and drew from his or her expressions an enormous range of human emotions. While one heard the voice of Archie, one was watching the detailed, intimate reactions of Edith. Or the reverse might be true. As Edith chattered in the background, the camera would scan Archie's face for every nuance of emotion — raised eyebrows, incredulity, astonishment, tenderness, exasperation. The language of gesture and facial expression was both touching and funny in one scene, as Edith tried to discuss the facts of life with Gloria on the day of her wedding. Somehow communication was portrayed without any sustained conversation — merely Gloria's well-chosen phrases and the camera's concentration on Edith's nervous, shy gestures and her intense look of helplessness.

Throughout the long-running series all of the characters developed, but perhaps Edith's growth is most relevant to a discussion of secular icons. Her character, in the early days of the program, was a negative model. While she was the stabilizing force in the family, she was consistently depicted in a subservient role. Later, Edith changed both in appearance and in the life she began to lead. The hairdo was less wispy, the motions around the house less frenetic. Edith eventually moved into a working world of her own.

The episodes that dealt with the temporary separation of Edith and Archie gave new depth to both characters. Archie, feeling lonely while Edith was away at work, called on a waitress. While nothing more than a waltz and a kiss ensued, his inability to be truthful with Edith compounded the trouble. Edith responded with despair and dismay at Archie's attempt to deceive her. Finally getting the truth from him, she rushed out the door in tears, lamenting that the one thing she could always count on was Archie, and now she couldn't count on him anymore. Eventually, through the mediating efforts of Mike and Gloria, they were brought face to face, though they were not speaking. Unreconciled, they nevertheless went back home together, where Edith announced she would sleep in the children's old room. Reconciliation came about later in the evening when Edith talked with Archie on the front porch. In this conversation there was a new, hitherto unexpressed quality of autonomy in Edith Bunker. She did not want to let the incident keep them apart for the rest of their lives, but she told Archie she didn't miss him as much as she thought she would. When she thought about him she missed him, but when she was busy, she thought about a lot of other things — and there were lots of other things to think about. She reflected that she used to think that Archie was the only thing she could count on, but now that "ain't true"; the something else she could count on now was herself. They repeated wedding vows, with the amendment that Edith would take Archie as her lawful wedded husband until she "can't take him no more." The comic element flourished again at the end when Edith's shrill voice awakened the neighborhood as she joyously belted out "How much do I love you . . ." In the face of shouting, protesting neighbors, Archie joined loudly, defiantly, in the second verse.

Edith and Archie are certainly figures far from the saints' images in the traditional icons. Those solemn, elongated, beatific countenances were sacred objects of veneration for people who believed in a greater supernatural order. The images of Edith and Archie are more like the icons Norman Rockwell created for early twentieth-century Americans. The Bunker household produced symbols of particular kinds of human action and beliefs in the secular, technological, democratic world of the 1970s. Whether viewers reacted positively or negatively to the characters, *All in the Family* embodied certain social values and conflicts, and, at the very least, made them accessible for public debate and reflection.

Unlike the Bunkers, TV families in other series have been comfortable, middle-class people who generally have problems that can be worked out in the course of an hour's program. Their economic status, relative domestic tranquillity and lifestyle are similar to those depicted in magazine and television advertising. Consider, for example, the visions of the good life conjured up on *Eight Is Enough*. The Bradford home has a spacious, suburban elegance with back and front lawns, an ample drive, and a garage with plenty of space for cars, work, and garden tools. There are references to neighbors, but one doesn't actually see any of their houses. Lush green plants and trees apparently screen one house from another. Inside, the Bradfords' rooms are large and well furnished, with lots of paintings and plants. Upstairs are bedrooms and bathrooms, and, though there is some doubling up in the rooms, no one seems cramped or uncomfortable. Downstairs, the kitchen and dining room are gathering places for the family; the study where Tom Bradford occasionally works is the setting for private conferences with one or more of the children.

Tom, the father, a newspaperman, is sole provider for the large household. Abby, his young second wife, is independent and high-spirited, exerting a leadership in the family that sometimes makes the father's decision making seem hesitant or conservative. Together they provide a broad, supportive base for all their children, some of whom are in their twenties. Even the oldest son, David, who is married, retains strong ties with the family.

Weekly shows frequently maintain two or three plots. These run parallel through the entire episode and are interwoven visually, with quick cuts back and forth to move the individual stories to a final resolution. The Bradford household itself remains the fixed center, providing equilibrium for the motion and interaction of the dramatic sequences. Through the interrelated plots the activities of the various family members point up simple moral lessons and demonstrate the solid supportive role of the family. In one episode David, the married son, became concerned about his working wife, Janet, who, he thought, was devoting too much time to her work. He further suspected she might be fooling around with her colleague in the law firm. A parallel motif involved Elizabeth, one of the daughters, who had just broken up with her boyfriend. She started going out with her brother's best friend, Ernie, and this worried Tommy who was very protective of his sister. Finally, the third motif centered on Nicholas, the youngest, and in many ways the most popular, character who got bored with his lifestyle after he had played at the house of his young black friend, Jackson.

As the stories developed, other Bradford family members were drawn into the action. David consulted with his dad who encouraged honesty and open communication between him and Janet. Tommy fretted about his sister and Ernie, and he and his father waited up for her when she returned home late one night. Dad also worried about Nicholas playing in "that part of town" but was assured by Abby that Nicholas should have a wide range of friends and experiences. The three stories moved quickly along, interspersed with commercials and, by the end of the hour, all was resolved. David and Janet had learned something new about honesty and mutual trust; Elizabeth made it clear that she was only friends with Ernie; Jackson had helped Nicholas see and appreciate his own family in a new way.

While the setting, dress, education, and characters reinforce the concept of the good life of a suburban family, many of the issues depicted in the episodes explore changing attitudes about family roles. The daughters of Tom Bradford show as much, if not more, independence as the sons. Lee Rich, the show's executive producer, has commented on the "realism" in some of the episodes:

> The oldest daughter decided she was in love with a young man. She went off and lived with him for several weeks before she returned home. . . The network had wanted the daughter to say she came back home because she now believes in marriage. That's ridiculous. The reason she came back was that she wasn't ready for it yet. Maybe next time, she says. I told ABC I wouldn't do the series unless I could do it honestly.[4]

Further, the stepmother, Abby, plays a real leadership role in the family. It is she who calms Tom Bradford's fears about his youngest child's exposure to a very different kind of social situation.

The dominant value that comes through all of the weekly episodes is the unwavering family loyalty and mutual, nurturing love. The affections may be tested and stretched, but there is unfailing forgiveness, and the family bond is never really broken. This aspect of the show tilts it perhaps toward "unrealism." But the producer, Bob Jacks, thinks that part of the show's appeal is precisely that it *"isn't real."*

> All across the country, people see the Bradfords and wish their own family were as happy and close knit as we are. This is what people wish life were like.[5]

For many persons, however, the nuclear family is not the only matrix for the expression of family norms. Social change inevitably brings changes in the concept of the family. While it was primarily the nuclear family or the widowed parent and children that represented TV households in earlier years, the single, divorced parent became a respectable head of the household later on in the 1970s. *One Day at a Time*, first broadcast in December 1975, popularized the concept of a single, di-

vorced woman who could successfully cope with her own life
and also function responsibly as a mother of two daughters.

Ann Romano of *One Day at a Time* has portrayed the difficulties
of being a divorcée, mother, professional woman, and head of
household

Ann Romano, divorced after seventeen years of marriage,
found, in her home town of Indianapolis, an apartment for herself and her two teen-age daughters, Julie and Barbara. Like
other family shows, the action focused mainly on the home itself — a small apartment with kitchen and dining area separated by a countertop. This space flowed into a small living
room with modern furniture. The girls shared a room that
looked cramped, and Ann had a bedroom to herself. The entire
apartment had a variety of pictures, posters, and knickknacks
on the wall for a homey touch. The building superintendent

and handyman, Dwayne Schneider, had a special protective attitude toward the girls, since Ms. Romano had no male figure around to look after them. Schneider's cultivated macho image — tattoo, T-shirt, tool belt around his waist — and his bravado set him apart in taste and class from the Romano family. While there was no chance of romance between him and Ann, he became, through his affection and concern for the group, a member of the family.

The show depicted with dignity and honesty the complicated, often painful, day-to-day problems of divorced parents: the sense of conflicting loyalties that children have toward their parents; the difficulties that a single parent has in maintaining discipline and authority, especially with teen-age children; and the woman's struggle to work as a professional, and at the same time do justice to her role as mother. The series explored some of the toughest situations between parents and teen-agers. There was great anxiety and heartache when Julie, the older daughter, ran off with her boyfriend in his van. In one episode Ann confronted them in a sleazy, rundown apartment and invited her daughter to return home — but to return with the rules of the game being understood. The family continued to grow: Julie eventually married, and Ann persisted as a character who nurtured the family group. As Ann Romano, Bonnie Franklin was uniquely successful in providing the model of divorcée, mother, mother-in-law, and professional woman in a situation comedy.

In another drama, *Family*, the Lawrences opened up for prime-time audiences a melodramatic and complex series of portrayals of family life. Its one-hour format allowed a searching exploration of problems that face contemporary families. The Lawrences were an affluent, middle-class family in Pasadena. The father, Doug, a successful, independent lawyer, was married to Kate, an equally strong, thoughtful, and intelligent person. They had three children of their own — Nancy, Willie, and Buddy — and an adopted child, Annie. They and their extended family faced crises of terminal illness, alcoholism, death, divorce, unwanted pregnancies, adoption, cancer, and accidents. Indeed, the circumstances of the Lawrence family seemed to many to follow the pattern of human travail and grief that characterized many of the daytime soap operas. What distinguished the Lawrences, however, was the artful portrayal of each member of the family as a thinking individual who could thoughtfully explore ethical issues and action. Through these thorough examinations of value questions, complex sets of options and alternative attitudes were developed. There were no quick fixes or easy resolutions.

When the series opened, Nancy, the older daughter, was facing the ordeal of an unfaithful husband and the question of divorce. When she discovered that she was pregnant, one of the episodes dealt with the question of abortion. As Nancy seriously contemplated an abortion, Kate, her mother, persistently and compassionately opposed it. In the course of their discussion Kate stressed the empathy she felt. She revealed that she also had once faced an unwanted pregnancy. Together she and Doug had made the decision to have the child and had been very glad for their decision. Doug, the father, however, became concerned that Kate was exerting pressure on Nancy. He felt that his daughter faced many more painful experiences as a single parent than Kate or he had faced when they were trying to make their own decision. Such different circumstances limited Kate's perspective. As the many sides of the question were explored, the viewer could readily perceive that *any* answer involved some kind of suffering. In this situation, the confrontation with grief was unavoidable. The conclusion was that Kate and Doug had to trust Nancy to make her own decision with the knowledge that the family was there to support her, whatever she decided to do. Nancy decided to have the baby.

Much later, in a kind of corresponding episode, the mother, Kate, faced the danger and perplexity of a menopausal pregnancy. The children and Doug were concerned about the well-being of Kate and the child. The younger daughter, Buddy, reacted in anger and in fear at the thought of allowing the pregnancy to continue. In spite of the family turmoil, Kate decided to go through with the pregnancy. After her miscarriage, what the viewer remembers most vividly is the real grief the older Kate experienced at the loss of her unborn child.

These issues and others examined in the series could easily have lent themselves to sensationalism. But the tasteful, scrupulous introspection and exploration of the issues by the major characters underscored the pathos of the human situation. The series dealt with the no-win situations that persons often face. But, whatever the dilemma, the family provided the opportunity for deliberation and decision making.

Although the Bradford, Romano, and Lawrence families had differing family situations, their socioeconomic and cultural orientations toward professional vocations and success were similar. Their lifestyles and the ultimate harmonious resolutions of their difficulties blended happily with the people and products of the commercial sponsors. Their good looks and essentially good life were things to wish for, along with the station wagons and Bermuda vacations advertised during the shows.

Occasionally, families depicted on television do not conform to this storybook profile. *Skag*, a brief series of dramatic shows presented by NBC in the winter of 1980, portrayed a working-class family. Skag was head of a household that differed significantly from the middle-class affluence of the Bradfords or Lawrences. The larger environment was that of a poor community with none of the features of the suburban dream. The background consisted of simple, almost bleak, modestly furnished frame houses and neighborhoods of mobile homes. The plots explored some of the problems that face low-income families. In one episode Skag's daughter defied her father and moved in with a mill supervisor who treated women irresponsibly. The daughter, Patricia, also asserted her independence by pursuing a modeling career. Her relationship with Whalen, the mill supervisor, was tenuous because she really wanted the glamorous life of a model. In the long run Patricia failed to secure a genuine modeling career but was persuaded to go to New York with other aspirants under the sponsorship of a man who had assured them of opportunities for advancement. The father sensed the seedy future that was in store for his daughter, but felt helpless to do anything about it. The episode ended on a note of foreboding and grief.

While critics and some viewers talk often about the need for more realism in TV families, it is not clear how much could be tolerated by viewers. The realism in some of the long-running series seems to be tempered with considerable humor, and generally their problems are resolved. It could be argued that what most people experience in their day-to-day lives is without resolution, often sad, and with only thin threads of hope. It is unlikely that viewers would be attracted to programs where week after week they look at the painful family conflicts and crises confronted by the poor.

By contrast, the success of the weekly series *Dallas* suggests that viewers are fascinated by the calamities and sins of the super-rich. Week after week the Ewing family experiences newer and more convoluted intrigue, grief, and meanness. The fabulously wealthy family endures constant misery, and each episode seems to be energized with a Texas-style abundance of lust and vengeance. The opening camera shots play on the local symbols of power: the Dallas skyline, industries, oil derricks, and the great open spaces. The grandiose house that accommodates the three families is like a citadel, arrived at through long, private drives and surrounded by Ewing property as far as the eye can see.

The Ewing men dominate the show. Jock, the cowboy–rancher–oil man–scheming entrepreneur who has made all the money, presides over the clan. The "good" son, Bobby, has the frontier qualities of the old man but is basically decent, more like his mother. The other son, J.R., wears boots and a Western hat, but what one remembers about him are the smooth, elegant suits and his sleazy, villainous character. His avarice and hard-living, hard-loving ways keep the show resplendent in sin. Miss Ellie is Jock's wife — a matronly, tastefully dressed woman, never seen in an apron or work clothes. She reigns as the gracious, forgiving mistress of the Ewing compound. The other major women are J.R.'s wife, Sue Ellen; Bobby's wife, Pam; and Jock and Miss Ellie's granddaughter, Lucy. Their often disastrous personal circumstances are experienced with psychic, more than physical, disarray. They are unfailingly well groomed and stylishly attired. The good life of the Ewings is inexorably bound up with wealth, and huge sums are continuously spent in coping with alcoholism, nervous breakdowns, kidnappings, infidelity, and lawsuits.

Many persons have speculated on the audience appeal of *Dallas*. Some have argued that viewers like it because it shows that the very rich are themselves tormented and unhappy. Or perhaps it diverts attention from the inflation rate and fuel prices. Others reflect that it resembles the tales of gods and superhumans, which almost always include a personification of evil and disorder. The dirty tricks and treachery of the characters help to clarify and identify the heroes and good folks. Another view was offered by Michael Arlen in a *New Yorker* article in which he speculated about the unpredictability and destabilized quality of the characters in *Dallas*:

> Its characters don't so much lack manners as lack a stable relationship to manners. Young and old, new rich and old rich, good characters and bad characters share this stripped down, improvisational sensibility.[6]

The "behavioral improvisation," he suggests, may appeal to viewers because the destabilized characters bear a strong resemblance to ourselves.

When it comes to the simpler, old-fashioned values, viewers have to set the dial for shows that depict families in the American past. There one can find families who must do hard, often manual, work to make ends meet. Of all the TV families, the Waltons stand out strongly as a source of traditional ideas about right and wrong. Set in the years between the Depression and World War II, the show embodies some of the heroic principles that we like to think of as uniquely American — honesty, hard work, belief in God, fair play, patriotism, and cooperation. And, it is within the family that these convictions are first experienced.

The Walton family originally consisted of John and Olivia Walton, their seven children, and Grandma and Grandpa Walton. They were a rural family in the mountains of Virginia. Walton's Mountain was itself a steady reference throughout the series of unchanging and transcendent ideals that each member of the family discovered for himself or herself. It symbolized the physical and spiritual qualities that Grandma and Grandpa Walton had sought to instill in their children and that John and Olivia had transmitted to theirs. Over the years the Walton family on television grew and underwent changes. Viewers watched the children mature and assume new and independent roles. When Will Geer, the actor who played Grandpa Zed, died, the Waltons had to absorb their grief and reconstitute themselves as a family. When Grandma Walton had to fight her way back from a stroke, the show incorporated the heroism that the actress, Ellen Corby, was experiencing in real life. Grandma Walton had to learn to regain her equilibrium and speech after being incapacitated.

The Waltons presented social as well as personal history. Clustered around the radio the family listened to Roosevelt speak to the nation after Pearl Harbor. Later episodes brought them into the war years. For viewers who remember only the skepticism and disenchantment with patriotism during the Vietnam years, the show reconstructed from the past a different kind of patriotism. It also, in a later episode, combined the motifs of patriotism and racial prejudice. Mary Ellen, the eldest daughter, befriended a young Mexican-American soldier who was on leave from the navy, and was being taunted by local boys. In a scuffle, the young soldier hurt the arm of one of the locals. After he was taken in by the Waltons, it turned out that Mary Ellen's husband, who died in action, had saved the young soldier's life at Pearl Harbor. He had come to bring a medal and note from President Roosevelt honoring Mary Ellen's husband. During his visit with the family, Mary Ellen found that it was possible for her to emerge from her own grief and begin to love again. The young soldier learned a kind of patience and restraint in dealing with the bigots who maligned him. Confronted by their jeers, he was encouraged by Mary Ellen to count to ten. By so doing, he reversed the mood of anger and reminded them that they were all equals, fighting together against a common enemy. As they all shook hands, a joyous party ensued.

The Waltons persistently made storytelling about the American past dramatically interesting. Like later TV families, this one had its own crises, but the old principles saw the family through. *The Waltons* is a symbolic record of family life, more akin to the creations of Norman Rockwell than to the 1930s photos by Ben Shahn and Dorothea Lange. They bear little resemblance to the Woods or Gudgers described in James Agee and Walker Evans' *Let Us Now Praise Famous Men*, which presented the poor with dignity, though without the physical or spiritual power to overcome the system. In *The Waltons* the old-fashioned values and the strength they provide are portrayed for a contemporary audience. Only such a fictionalized family living in the shadow of history and of Walton's Mountain could personify such principles.

At the opposite end of the spectrum from the Waltons and their values are the ethical embroilments portrayed in daytime soap operas. Over the years some of the longer-running series have developed inordinately complex human relationships that only devoted fans can decipher. Few prime-time shows can challenge the supremacy of the soap operas in the sheer quantity of human value questions that have saturated these fictional families. In fact, the soap opera makes a very specialized use of the family metaphor. Because of the daily dramatization the shows can encompass not just one but a number of interrelated families. This leads to a complicated interweaving of births, marriages, sicknesses, divorces, lawsuits, infidelities, and reconciliations. The family environment alone cannot accommodate this rich fabric of human experience. To represent the intricacies and multiplicity of families in crises, it is necessary to include larger communal areas: innumerable offices of doctors, lawyers, psychiatrists, detectives, and the exciting spaces of the hospital — x-ray rooms, corridors, emergency wards, waiting rooms, operating rooms, and so on. These communal spaces, into which all the family crises overflow, eventually provide viewers with images of the entire community in which the families reside.

Informed critics say that soap operas confirm as well as question traditional moral values. According to some, soap operas actually inspire adherence to traditional codes of behavior. The wicked are indeed punished or live under unbearable social pressures. Critic Neil Shister even concludes that soap opera families argue for the triumph of innocence and decency:

> Innocence remains despite all. That's the final message one takes from the program before the last barrage of commercials promising that a clean wash or a platter of Oriental vegetables is the sure bet to make a family ecstatic. The pristine promise of youth might get sullied a little in Pine Valley, but it never gets eroded. . . There's no way you can watch for several weeks without getting involved. People get banged around in Pine Valley — most of them have hearts encased in several layers of scar tissue — but they pass through their bouts of tortured anxiety without shriveling up into emotional basket-cases. They are the inspirational icons of TV.[7]

But do they inspire by their perseverance and innocence? Probably not. They may enable viewers to empathize with a wide range of moral predicaments. Or they may lead viewers so deeply into an assortment of human grief and folly that they are hypnotized and at the same time somewhat relieved by the relatively uncomplicated state of their own family lives. Shister admits that part of the attraction of the soap operas is that the trials of the characters make one's own life seem simple by comparison: "When you turn off the set your own life seems like peaches-and-cream. Or at least Ready-Whip."[8]

The rhythm of the soap opera is significantly different from that of the weekly family series. The soaps are both more regulated and more open-ended. On the one hand, the sophisticated viewer can almost predict the commercial breaks and the previews for subsequent episodes. The soap opera fan is locked into a daily habit; the viewing becomes a kind of ritualistic experience. On the other hand, the daily rhythm of the programs allows a linear extension in the life of the fictionalized family that corresponds closely to the open-ended quality of life itself. Part of the fascination of the soap operas may be, in fact, their capacity to symbolize for viewers the unpredictability and openness of day-to-day living; people can identify with the characters who work through their fateful circumstances daily. Moreover, some of the long-running soap operas reflect and shape viewers' changing moral attitudes.

For television viewers, the family has always been a special kind of visual metaphor. It represents an immediate "world" of parents and children, but at the same time inevitably leads viewers into an awareness of the larger communities of neighborhood, city, state, and nation. Indeed, the size and environment of the family has been so convenient for presenting relationships on television that many shows — *The Mary Tyler Moore Show*, *M*A*S*H*, *The Lou Grant Show*, *The White Shadow*, and others — seem analogous to family groups. Out of a large organization — newspaper office, military hospital, high school — certain key individuals interact with each other in such a way that viewers see them as a kind of family. Sometimes the family image is even applied to an entire network. When CBS observed its fiftieth anniversary, the network "family" gathered together. Presided over by Walter Cronkite, one of the hosts of the occasion, stars of the past and present celebrated as though at a family reunion. In another instance, during this nation's Bicentennial, Cronkite led viewers on a national tour, at the end of which he delivered a fatherly tribute to our pluralistic national family.

Roots, one of the most widely viewed family portrayals in television history, was built around a particular family's history. Developing a sense of ethnic origin and destiny, the series was a significant step in television, inspiring the black family with a world of its own. *Roots* became a spectacular icon with which the individual American Black could identify. Although some parts of the series were criticized for stereotyping whites, the lasting power of the production was its capacity to give to black Americans epic images of themselves. As an icon, it articulated myth in the best sense of the word — explaining who black Americans are, where they came from, and where they are going. *Roots* enabled the black American to have a sense of the whole of which the individual is a part.

Nature

Visually incomprehensible in its totality, the order of nature, like other concepts, may be symbolized in words and images. One may grasp some sense of the whole through a memorable experience of a natural phenomenon — a dramatic sunset on a lake or a mountain storm. In American culture nature has been an important source of public myth and imagery. Throughout this nation's history there have been countless persons whose most basic understanding of experience has been informed by the rhythms, spaces, and processes of nature — life and death, growth and decay, harmony and violence. The visual and emotional impact of nature has been expressed in work as varied as the topographical drawings of early explorers, the highly abstracted nature images of Georgia O'Keeffe, and Western films. When television incorporates aspects of nature, either as a major focus or as background for human dramatic action, it continues and transforms an important symbol that has very deep roots in American cultural history.

From the time that Europeans first beheld and walked into American forests, the terrain and its wildlife stimulated scientific curiosity and aesthetic pleasure. In the nineteenth century much of the American territory, unlike that of Europe, still had not been fully explored. The wildness and luxuriance of the continent lured naturalists like John James Audubon into remote areas to secure specimens and document visually the flora and fauna of the new Eden. Audubon's sketches and notations became the basic materials for lithographers. They adapted his sketches and produced exquisite color prints of bison, antelope, and unique birds. Adorning the walls of prosperous citizens, they became a nineteenth-century mass medium, reflecting the wonder of American nature.

Earlier, George Catlin had also been driven to explore life beyond the settled areas. But he had interests quite different from those of Audubon. His sketches, paintings, and journals depicted the life of the American Indians. Catlin traveled West to draw and paint the inhabitants in their native environment. His careful documentation of ritual experience, hunting techniques, and social customs became the basis for lithographic prints that were circulated in this country and in Europe. Seeing these prints, many Americans formed an understanding of the rituals and customs of a people whose life before colonization had been intertwined with nature.

While Catlin and Audubon saw nature as a subject for accurate representation, a number of nineteenth-century American landscape painters viewed nature from a distinctly theological perspective. Thomas Cole, for example, was one of the most verbally articulate landscapists. American nature, he observed, was a special privilege given to the artist — nature untouched from the time of Creation, a visible reference to the work of the Creator.[9] The painter was imbued with a sense of awe and wonder, and, in contemplating nature, became aware of transcendent being. Although Cole himself would have preferred to use Biblical and allegorical subjects in his paintings, the public responded more favorably to his landscapes. Cole's landscapes were a special kind of religious icon for predominantly Protestant America. In a country where nature was so very impressive and the Christian conviction of creation so powerful, landscape painting lent itself to theological reflection. Landscape was a meditative image that heightened the mystery of creation. From Cole to George Inness and Albert P.

Ryder, this interpretation persisted throughout the century. Styles and techniques underwent changes, but the religious overtones lingered on.

Other artists of that period dramatized the conquest of the wilderness. Although historians today are revising impressions of the Western frontier, many images of the nineteenth century showed the wilderness as a space of conquest and domestication. George Caleb Bingham's painting of Daniel Boone leading a band into the wilderness suggested just such a heroic mission. Lithographs by various artists offered images of conquest — prints depicting the hunting of buffalo and other wildlife — for popular consumption. Late in the century Remington provided *Harper's Weekly* with illustrations of cowboys and Western life that continued these motifs.

One of the most elaborate embodiments of the myth of conquest was a monumental piece of sculpture commissioned in 1837 for the Capitol. The basic motif of Horatio Greenough's design was a pioneer overpowering an Indian. Entitled *The Rescue*, the large sculpture showed a white man restraining an Indian, while to one side a woman and child cringed in fear. In the artist's own words, the work was intended to "convey the idea of the triumph of the whites over the savage tribes, at the same time that it illustrated the danger of peopling the country."[10]

In the twentieth century the technological revolutions in printing — which brought first, black and white, and later, color reproductions of photographs — opened up extraordinary opportunities for photographers and journalists to explore and document life processes and natural environments. Indeed, it is possible that the religious reverence for the American landscape in the nineteenth century was reborn in ecologically oriented photographers such as Ansel Adams. Nineteenth-century American landscape paintings and lithographs became the prototypes for the majestic color photos on Sierra Club posters and calendars and for the images in such magazines as the *National Geographic*.

Television programs have also used nature images, but in a

limited and selected way. In comparison to the family — which despite all its changes persists as a constant world in which humans interact — the world of nature seems very distant. For most Americans nature exists at the periphery of their experience. Unless they live in a farming community, they are somewhat insensitive to the vicissitudes of the natural order. Of course, they become aware of its power when they see news reports of natural disasters. But in the ordinary course of events, the city and suburban dwellers keep an eye on the weather reports to anticipate the fuel bill, transportation difficulties, or the possibility of a good day at the beach. Nature as an awesome, transcendent order within which human beings and all levels of life must be harmonized is a remote concept. Although ecologists and conservationists have urged us to see nature in ways other than exploitative, most people see the natural order as subservient to technology and human manipulation. Relatively few of us appreciate, for example, the Hopi Indians' sense of loss at seeing mountains desecrated by strip mining. Expediency dominates most of our thinking in the tradeoffs between nature and technology.

Television is witness to these shifts in our thinking about nature. The mystical aspect of nature, widely displayed in the work of many nineteenth-century American landscape artists, is only a faint motif in television today, if it appears at all. This failure may be due not only to a shift in our basic thinking about nature but also to the character of the medium itself. Still images, such as paintings and photographs, can and do inspire contemplative and sustained reflection upon nature as an awesome witness to the process of creation. The moving images of television, on the other hand, lend themselves more to storytelling and fast dramatic interaction.

Slight traces of the mystical interpretation of the natural order do occasionally appear on television in a simplified form. A few seasons ago, one weekly series, *The Life and Times of Grizzly Adams*, featured a hero who possessed a mystical kinship with the wilderness and its creatures. Living in the Western wilderness in the late nineteenth century, Grizzly Adams had fled the city when he was accused of a crime he had not committed. But his life in the wild was more than a refuge from the law. There he came to understand the ultimate harmony of all creatures and natural phenomena. One particular animal, Ben, a grizzly bear he had rescued as a cub, became his constant companion.

This series and the movie that preceded it were inspired by a real Grizzly Adams who left the East and spent years in the mountains. Although he was a hunter and a collector for zoos, he saved and cared for many of the animals. His TV counterpart was portrayed more as a simplified, mountain-man type, somewhat like St. Francis of Assisi. The fictitious Grizzly Adams had a way of communicating with all kinds of animals, and his insights and powers protected them from danger. His deep kinship lay with the elements — sun, storms, seasons, forests — and with the creatures who lived in the wild.

This show may have seemed shallow to some viewers, but it at least represented a superficial connection with a deeper strain of religious thought. Some small residue of a mystical view of creation and the harmony of its parts found concrete expression in the fictionalized and fantasized images of a mountain-man. More than that, this portrayal of a sentimentalized St. Francis possibly evoked the sympathy that even some Protestant Americans have felt for the saint who found his sisters and brothers among the creatures in nature.

Adventure, rather than aesthetic or religious contemplation, has been the dominant symbol of the wilderness on television. The Western adventure, in fact, has become an American specialty, and in the 1950s and 1960s many TV series used the literary and visual qualities that had been developed in earlier films. Because of its popularity and history, this genre has been carefully analyzed by both film and television critics. Therefore, I want simply to call attention to the particular values that were unique to the wilderness metaphor in the TV Western.

While the space of the family has been a small, protected area of support and nurture, the space of the wilderness put human beings on trial and tested the stamina of individuals and communities. Sometimes the sheer physical experience of crossing mountains and deserts became occasions for heroism, endurance, or defeat. But, more often, the wilderness was symbolized as frontier, the boundary of civilization. There the adversary was not primarily an untamed nature but the forces that resisted the claims of society. In his discussion of the Western formula, John Cawelti has pointed out that the frontier provided a "fictional justification for enjoying violent conflicts and the expression of lawless force without feeling that they threatened the values or the fabric of society."[11] The frontier presented the space and occasion for locating the "other" who was a threat to oneself and one's kind. In the absence of formal myths, which provide socially acceptable images of the forces of darkness and the forces of light, the outlaws and Indians filled that void for some American storytellers and imagemakers.

One popular TV series of the late 1950s, *Wagon Train*, used the concept of wilderness as adversary, and dramatized the struggles that threatened the civilizing activities of those moving westward. Each year the series featured a California-bound wagon train that started out in the fall from St. Joseph, Missouri. Every episode in the series moved the wagon train farther west, crossing the Great Plains, deserts, and the awesome Rocky Mountains. Along the way the wagon train encountered lawless gunmen, Indians, or natural disasters. As the television season ended, the wagon train reached its California goal, having survived the many different threats encountered on the journey.

One could perceive in this series and others like it how TV Westerns were different from their movie counterparts. Images on the small home screen could never present the astonishing grandeur of the West in the way that film makers had done on the large movie screens. The small screen simply could not accommodate views of the spectacular terrain that John Ford, for example, had used in *Stagecoach*. Scenes in that film showed vividly how dwarfed and insignificant the horse-drawn coach could be when viewed against the great vistas of the open western spaces. The dramatic terrain — craggy mountains, expansive emptiness — projected on large movie screens, seemed literally to engulf the audience. For their most dramatic effects, the television Westerns concentrated on the full face of the wagon master, or zoomed in with tight shots of terrified horses. The detailed contours of human faces and animal forms carried on the small screen the power of proportionality, texture, and intensity that the large vistas had produced on the movie screens.

The adversaries faced on the frontier contributed to the formation of a particular kind of American hero. Whether confronting the threats of nature, outlaw or Indian, the hero was one who had to maintain or restore order. In his discussion of the Western, Horace Newcomb has observed that its central problem is the establishment of order.

> The Western hero is the man who brings order. He may be an Indian fighter, a marshal, a cavalry officer, a gunfighter, or a wagon master. Unlike the helpless townspeople or untrained immigrants from peaceful Ohio, he possesses the proper skills with which to cope with the threats of savagery. Indeed, he is necessarily tainted with savagery himself; he is able to bear arms and willing to use them.[12]

But the Western hero, while willing to use violence to maintain order, did so only reluctantly. Few TV heroes have been able to personify both that sense of power and of restraint as vividly as Matt Dillon, the marshal in *Gunsmoke*. The six-foot, seven-inch stature and the somber, stalwart face of James Arness dramatically portrayed what John Cawelti has referred to as the "reluctance, control and elegance" of the Western hero.

> Unlike the knight, the cowboy hero does not seek out combat for its own sake and he typically shows an aversion to the wanton shedding of blood. Killing

is an act forced upon him and he carries it out with the precision and skill of a surgeon and the careful proportions of an artist.[13]

Matt Dillon, the somber, stalwart marshal in *Gunsmoke*, personifies the Western hero

Gunsmoke was the longest running Western in American television history. It lasted twenty years, from September 1955 to September 1975, and for four of those years was the top-rated television program. The popularity and longevity of this and other Western series suggest the television viewers' endorsement of the public symbols and mythology that Westerns supplied. The frontier provided a mythological space in which forces of good and evil, of order and disorder, engaged in mortal combat. From this struggle for right and order emerged a special kind of hero who had a public obligation to establish order, resorting to violence only when there was no alternative.

Although Westerns from the 1950s and 1960s, such as *Gunsmoke* and *Bonanza*, are currently rerun by some stations in the late afternoon, prime-time dramatizations of the struggle for order mostly use symbols of technology, the city, and outer space. One series, however, experimented with a curious mixture of the metaphors of wilderness, machine, and city. The show *Hagen* took its name from the hero himself, a mountain-man turned detective. The opening shots combined views of the wilderness mountains, rafting, and rapids and panoramas of San Francisco, a city of bustling action. While the plots of the show often took the hero away from the urban haunts into the wilder, more remote terrain, Hagen actually worked as a troubleshooter for a lawyer in the city.

His allegiance to the wilderness and his at-homeness there became apparent through references to his tracking ability, archery skills, backpacking, and his preference for the outdoors. But it was largely his appearance that continually communicated to the viewer that this was a nature type, not a city type. Hagen's tough, lean physique was outfitted in rugged, tight trousers, hiking boots, red plaid jacket, and down vest, and occasionally a lambskin jacket. His inclination to dwell close to nature was also evident in his mode of transportation. Though it was not a white horse, Hagen maneuvered through the streets of San Francisco in a machine that is often indispensable in wild, roadless territory — a white, open-top jeep.

The plots of the show frequently took Hagen outdoors. One could see how well he operated in his natural environment — scaling rocks, crawling, scrambling, gracefully and instinctively moving through mountainous and wooded areas. But his training and skills in outdoor living also helped him deal with the lawbreakers in the city. He could discover and deliver ex-Nazi criminals to the proper authorities or use his bare hands to round up a corrupt businessman and sheriff in a neighboring small town. The tough, compassionate, soft-spoken, sophisticated mountain-man moved easily between wilderness and city, maintaining order. His loyalties arose from his deep relationship to nature, but the action took place in the city. The mysteries and problems in which he became involved stemmed not from nature but from a complex technological culture.

The Ingalls, moving westward in *Little House on the Prairie*, dramatize American images of family and wilderness

Unlike *Hagen*, which combined wilderness, machines, and city metaphors, another series, *Little House on the Prairie*, combined wilderness and family. Every week the opening shots introduced strong, familiar symbols: a single covered wagon moving westward, detailed shots of the radiant faces of a young husband and wife — all in brilliant sunlight. Their children were seen running, laughing, tumbling airily down a sloping, luxuriant spring-green meadow.

The pioneering couple, Charles and Caroline Ingalls, moved from Kansas to homestead in Minnesota. For several years viewers followed the family through the good and lean years of living and growing together. The three daughters, Mary, Laura, and Carrie, matured into distinct personalities; a fourth daughter, Grace, was born and a son, Albert, was adopted. As a family they cultivated the land, faced the uncertainties of seasons and crops, and became part of their nearby village, Walnut Grove. At one point they left the farm for the frontier city of Winoka in the Dakota Territory, and later in a memorable episode they and the neighbors who had moved with them returned to their Minnesota homesteads.

The show's physical and historical setting promoted the kind of character portrayal that, as in *The Waltons*, expresses the good life and homespun virtues. In both the small village of Walnut Grove and on the farm, life was work centered. Everyone was always performing chores of one kind or another. Children had specific tasks to accomplish around the house and on the farm. While the women had an independent spirit, their social status was defined almost entirely by their roles as wives and mothers. Laura, one of the daughters, wanted very much to be a schoolteacher and, when she turned sixteen, her chance came to try it out. But she also wanted to grow up and marry Almanzo.

Understanding and love were ever present in the Ingalls family. The reasonable and compassionate parents were at the same time authoritative. Communication was expected and practiced by all, and through close-knit devotion they weathered their tragedies — among them, the blindness of the oldest daughter, Mary, from scarlet fever. Mary went to a school for the blind and eventually married her teacher Adam Kendall, and they started a family of their own.

The small village, Walnut Grove, introduced other kinds of relationships. One often repeated symbol was the little white, steepled church. There the townspeople worshiped, and there Mary and Adam were married. But the religious motif was not confined to worship, weddings, and funerals. There was a general sense that people's lives were touched in particular ways by their faith. In one episode blind Mary struggled from an overturned stagecoach to go for help. Groping and feeling her way, she finally fell in prairie brush utterly exhausted and lost. But some glasses she had been carrying picked up the sun's rays, setting a grass fire that attracted the attention of rescuers. For Mary and her family, with their old-fashioned faith, it was a miracle.

Little House on the Prairie combined images of hardy, God-fearing settlers with spectacular vistas of the hills and plains they traversed and cultivated. Women in bonnets and men chopping wood were silhouetted against green and gold landscapes.

Similarly, Walt Disney used nature as a backdrop in his productions. Beginning in 1954 Disney created adventure shows and nature documentaries that even today occupy a place on prime-time television. In the shows *Frontierland* and *True Life Adventureland* Disney tapped the persistent love of nature felt by many Americans. Through the televised interpretations of myth and history, the Disney studios turned Davy Crockett into a national hero for millions of young Americans in the mid-1950s. The theme song, "The Ballad of Davy Crockett," was a hit record, and unfortunately, the popularity of the raccoon cap took its toll on the raccoon population. The three Davy Crockett episodes were so successful that Disney used other Western and frontier heroes for television programs. Later Disney developed nature-oriented stories. Some were documentaries that dealt entirely with natural phenomena. Others were stories that combined the adventures of special animals and their young friends. From the Disney studios came such stars as Lefty, the Ding-a-Ling Linx; Ida, the Offbeat Eagle; Salty, the Hijacked Harbor Seal; Joker, the Amiable Ocelot; and many others.

In addition to the nature and adventure shows, Walt Disney and his successors in the Disney productions have also transformed wildlife motifs into popular cultural symbols. Ever since the introduction of the animated cartoon "Steamboat Willie" in 1928, Disney's anthropomorphized creatures have plasticized and packaged sentiments and attitudes about nature. It is difficult to conceive of a child or adult encountering a bear or raccoon in the woods unencumbered by the prototypical visions of popular animation. These creatures have, indeed, taken on the magnitude of nationally and internationally known symbols; Disneyland and Disneyworld have become sacred sites for millions of American and foreign pilgrims.

In popularizing nature and adventure and in creating cartoon characters such as Mickey Mouse and Donald Duck, Walt Disney and others capitalized on that deeply rooted interest in wilderness and animal life. The images entertained and instructed a young audience, but did not communicate profound theological visions of American nature. Neither did they portray the more tragic conflicts between nature and technology that have arisen in the twentieth century. Moreover, although these programs were directed largely toward youthful audiences, their interpretations of nature have, unfortunately, slipped into our adult consciousness and have become an easy, superficial way of thinking about wildlife.

Today the animated images of animals easily lend themselves to advertising almost any product. The Saturday morning programs blend the imaginary creatures and the cereals they promote. These little humanlike creatures also help us celebrate solemn religious festivals. Rudolph the Red-Nosed Reindeer signals Advent and Christmas and the Easter Bunny annually explains how colored eggs came to be.

The older sense of the awe and wonder in nature cannot be found in these animated images but, paradoxically, in the images that advanced technology has made possible. Intricate instruments propelled into outer space send back pictures of the moons of Jupiter. Programs like *The Invisible World* astonished the viewer with images of the motion of atoms or of patterns of energy that the human eye could never perceive. Following the lead of explorer-artists like Audubon and Catlin, the producers of these programs continue the nineteenth-century spirit of discovery and documentation.

Scientific discoveries have opened up new perspectives on deep recesses of the universe and revealed the incomprehensible dimensions of matter and energy. Thus the *Nova* programs and those of the National Geographic Society, for example, move far beyond the spaces of American nature into unseen and unexplored regions of the cosmos. *Nova: Universe* may even have started viewers thinking about the origin of our universe. While dealing with scientific theories and evidence, there was no attempt to "square" religious mythology with scientific theory. Yet, the very question of the origin of the universe pointed up to serious viewers certain areas in which myth and science overlap. When exploring the question of origin, an old awe is stimulated by a new visual form.

Sometimes natural phenomena are seen in a new way on television. ABC's live coverage of the eclipse of the sun brought moving pictures into the homes of persons who otherwise never could have seen a total eclipse. Certainly, many flipped the dial quickly to their favorite soap operas, and some didn't turn on the television set at all. But others saw this live coverage with sensitivity and appreciation for the rhythms and wonders of nature. This telecast made it possible for people to witness an unusual natural phenomenon and to share sentiments of wonder with other viewers who could not be physically present at those sites.

Perhaps more stirring were those universally memorable views of the earth sent back by the astronauts. As inhabitants of that spherical mass, we saw our dwelling place get smaller and smaller as the space ships moved toward the moon. We also saw telecasts "live from the moon." Such images would have been spatially and technologically inconceivable to nineteenth-century explorers of the American terrain. But now, technology provides images that enable viewers to contemplate both the wonders of science and of creation.

Machine

The term *technology* suggests an immense system whose magnitude is difficult, if not impossible, to comprehend. Though one cannot see the "whole" of technology, aspects of that vast order are symbolized by both objects and images: automobiles and images of automobiles, a computer and a picture of a computer chip, space ships and telecast space explorations. Most Americans have come to accept technology in the same way that the natural order is accepted, as an important world within which experience is measured and evaluated. This world has its own particular kinds of mythology and imagery, which are shaped and reflected by television. As visual metaphor and as object of veneration the machine is a "used" symbolic form, deeply embedded in American culture. Television builds upon a tradition in which technology and the vast proliferation of its products have provided both motivation and visual context for many kinds of images.

In the nineteenth century, Horatio Greenough, a sculptor and art theorist, was one of the first American artists to develop what might be considered a machine aesthetic. His concept of the machine and its beauty was based upon the relationship of an object's shape, composition, and materials to its use. Distinguishing between what he considered "expressive" and "functional" forms, Greenough admonished artists not to imitate the forms of Greek art, but to turn to nature for inspiration and models. In fact, the key words in his writings were drawn from biology: "process," "development," "organization," and "adaptation." Nature, in Greenough's pre-electronic technology, would guide artists and craftsmen: "Let us consult nature, and in the assurance that she will disclose a mine richer than ever was dreamed of by the Greeks, in art as well as in philosophy."[14] Objects made by human hands were to be, like the forms of nature, so carefully designed that there was nothing extraneous, no single part unnecessary to the cohesion of the whole. Greenough's remarks on the relation of form to function were directed toward architecture, but to make his points he referred to objects perfected by the technology of his time.

> Observe a ship at sea! Mark the majestic form of her hull as she rushes through the water, observe the graceful bend of her body, the gentle transmission

> from round to flat, the grasp of her keel, the leap
> of her bows, the symmetry and rich tracery of her
> spars and rigging, and those grand wind muscles, her
> sails.[15]

While nature gave designers the principles for architecture
and useful objects, Greenough and other nineteenth-century
thinkers conceived of nature itself in a religious dimension.
His theories of functionalism and the kind of technological
beauty he envisioned were interwoven with a theological con-
ception of the natural order:

> If there be any principle of structure more plainly in-
> culcated in the works of the Creator than all others,
> it is the principle of unflinching adaptation of forms
> to functions.[16]

Neither technology nor nature was autonomous; they were
bound together in the transcendent order of Creation, which
informed technology and the processes of human invention.

Ironically, Greenough's own work does not reflect his theory. Most of his sculpture was portraiture and the monumental
pieces he did for the Capitol were expressive — representing
the sentiments of a people — rather than functional. There
was, however, a community, the Shakers, which in its architecture and invented objects carried out almost to perfection
his aesthetic dictum. The technology of the Shakers was confined to the tools, objects, and architecture of a pastoral rather
than urban environment. Within these limits the Shakers
developed the aesthetic of functionalism to an extraordinary
degree. Using the visual elements and principles of light, proportion, and space, they produced objects that strangely anticipated the machine aesthetic of the twentieth century. Their
sensitivity to the uses and limitations of natural materials
brought about works of incomparable beauty. Even their tools,
which demonstrated Greenough's principles of organization
and adaptation, appear as exquisite sculptural forms. For the
Shakers, as for Greenough and many nineteenth-century

Americans, the order of technology was contained within the larger order of nature. Both the processes of nature and the processes of human inventiveness were subject to a transcendent order within which there was no conflict.

Conflict between nature and technology, so familiar to the twentieth century, did not appear in popular art either. Currier and Ives prints are a rich source of images of machines — steamboats, locomotives, and fire engines — that apparently fascinate the public. Thomas Cole hated the railroad and the way the tracks were cutting into his wilderness, but Currier and Ives specialized in portraying some of these machines. The most interesting aspect of these images is that they were almost always, except for the fire engine, set in a romantic, natural context: a locomotive moves through a pass in a mountainous terrain under a bright shining moon; a steamboat races on the Mississippi sending great clouds of smoke into a starlit sky. The conflict between the natural environment and machines, between human dignity and technology was yet to come.

Early twentieth-century artists who used images of the machine as major metaphors in their work were less articulate theorists than Greenough. However, in 1901 Frank Lloyd Wright expressed one modern attitude toward the machine and technology:

> A hope has grown stronger with the experience of
> each year, amounting now to a gradually deepening
> conviction that in the Machine lies the only future
> of art and craft — as I believe, a glorious future; that
> the Machine is, in fact, the metamorphosis of
> ancient art and craft: that we are at last face to face
> with the machine — the modern Sphinx.[17]

Like Greenough and the Shakers, Wright preferred those forms shaped by function and materials. He even believed that with careful selection of materials and functional design beautiful objects could be machine-made.

There were photographers and painters, as well, whose

images of machines emphasized the beauty of functional forms. Charles Sheeler, a painter and photographer, best exemplified the maker of the machine icon in the early twentieth century. After some early experiments in cubist landscapes, he discovered in the 1920s the iconography of technology, which became the most persistent imagery in his work. Specifically, his photographs of the Ford River Rouge plant were both an artistic and commercial success. The clarity of structure and elegant organization of parts to whole was the same that had been expressed by Greenough and practiced by the Shakers.

Sheeler grasped the significance of machines and factories as American public symbols and self-consciously used them in his paintings and photographs. If his images have a clarity and austere beauty, with no hint of pollution or destruction of the environment, it is because he saw in technology a secular substitute for a transcendent order of being. For Sheeler, images, objects, and architecture visibly embodied a symbolic order. His comments after viewing Chartres cathedral are important:

> Chartres is the flower of a time, having its roots in the deeper emotions of a people who sought the relief of outer expression. Religion was a great mass consciousness, and by the projection of the cathedral the welcome opportunity was given them. Every age manifests itself by some external evidence. In a period such as ours when only a comparatively few individuals seem to be given to religion, some form other than the Gothic cathedral must be found. Industry concerns the greatest numbers — it may be true, as has been said, that our factories are our substitute for religious expression.[18]

Sheeler's iconography and his persistent sensitivity to the machine aesthetic were apparent throughout his career. Even at a time in American art history when the nonrepresentational claimed the loyalties of major artists, Sheeler continued to employ in his work the imagery of the machine and of industry. It was more than an aesthetic for him; the images were icons, symbols of a larger whole of which he was a part.

Today advertising gives us many of our images of technology and its products. After World War II elaborate full-color reproductions became commonplace. Since then, we have become accustomed to a dense visual environment of ads. The machines and industrial sites that inspired Sheeler's paintings and photographs are now depicted everywhere — in magazines, newspapers, posters, and billboards. Automobiles, refrigerators, sewing machines, and appliances do more than promote sales; these images shape our perceptions of technology, production, and consumption.

Such symbolization of technology has been appropriated readily by television. In commercials the machines are no longer static: the viewers see what seems like the real thing. On the TV screen one sees the machines in action: the automobiles racing down the road, the power saws cutting down trees, the washing machines turning out whiter than white loads of laundry. And while commercials keep machines constantly before viewers, many programs, especially some of the adventure series, structure their action around automobiles, motorcycles, and airplanes. Investigators, police, and undercover agents depend upon the automobile to link their actions. Try to imagine, for example, Charlie's Angels maneuvering without machines. Apartments, courtrooms, scenes of the crime, police stations, showdown sites are woven together by recurring shots of wheels, drivers, turns, screeches, and crashes.

When nature does not seem to be the suitable setting for dramatic action and there is no family to which the hero or heroine continually relates, it is the machine that frequently becomes the constant against which plot and the weekly changing environments are played. In one program, *CHiPs*, featuring two young California Highway Patrol officers, action on motorcycles was the persistent motif. *TV Guide* described the program:

In this Family Viewing Time police series, the heroes
won't be drawing their guns. What *will* they be
doing? Weaving in and out of freeway traffic on their
motorcycles, thwarting an auto-theft ring, weaving
in and out of thruway traffic, rescuing a pretty girl
who's pinned inside an overturned car, weaving in
and out of traffic, collaring a thug who preys on
stranded motorists, weaving in and out, recapturing
monkeys that have escaped from a truck,
weaving. . . [19]

Another show, *The Dukes of Hazzard,* was built around automobile gymnastics. The plot didn't matter; anything that got a
chase going would do. The action took place in a small, country community where everybody knew everybody. The good
old Duke boys were modern Robin Hoods on wheels who
harassed the corrupt law officer, Boss Hogg, and his fumbling
deputies. But the real "stars" of the show were the automobiles, pickup trucks, and police patrol cars that dominated the
action. The Duke boys would take a running leap, glide gracefully through the open windows into the front seat of their car,
the General Lee, and the action began. The chases were rarely
confined to roads; the vehicles tore across fields and meadows
and took daring leaps over rock walls. They stirred up great
smoke screens of dust, crashed through barricades, drove into
trees, rolled over, landed upright, and roared off again in yet
another great cloud of dust.

While the Duke boys were part of a warm, clanlike family
headed by Uncle Jesse, the values of the show did not derive
from an examination of the complex human relations within a
family. Rather, the family context simply gave a clean-cut,
folksy image to people who get their kicks out of the acrobatics
and the care and nurture of the automobile. The dramatic action of the show could be compared to certain kinds of auto
races and to the dare-devil adventure of persons like Evil
Knevil. But the Dukes, portrayed as simple, strong, honest,
family-loving country boys, gave a down-home image to stunt

driving and entertained viewers who were fascinated by auto-mobile gymnastics, collisions, and adventure.

Television has also appropriated the popular genre of science fiction and its speculative, imaginative visions of tech-nology. Between 1949 and 1955 *Captain Video and His Video Rangers* introduced children to space machines, adversaries from other planets, and futuristic images of technology. There was the Atomic Rifle, which could blow up everything in earthly or other planetary space. And Captain Video used a Cosmic Ray Vibrator to shake the enemies into compliance with right order and justice. Tobor, the indestructible robot, helped Captain Video work against the forces of evil. After *Captain Video and His Video Rangers*, *Star Trek* took viewers into outer space. Exploring that mysterious realm and trans-porting supplies to colonialists who were making their homes there, *Star Trek* brought to television more complex science fiction than ever before. It combined the fantasy of unknown and undiscovered creatures with well-known observations about human nature. Embattled encounters in a future space and time included aspects of social conflicts experienced in the late 1960s.

A generation later, the children of those who watched Cap-tain Video tuned in to *Battle Star Gallactica* and *Buck Rogers in the 25th Century*. The concepts of space travel and tech-nology in the 1970s were influenced considerably by the actual trips made into outer space for scientific tests and exploration. The viewers who watched these newer science fiction adven-ture series had also seen on their TVs the giant computer con-soles and the blinking lights at NASA control center. And, of course, these programs were also spurred on by the great popu-larity of the movie *Star Wars* with its new film techniques and special effects.

The science fiction television series have featured world views, heroes, and questions that may seem less fantastic now than they were in the years of Captain Video. In the twenty-fifth-century world of Buck Rogers, television viewers don't see much grass or hear references to spring and summer.

Instead, they are accustomed to the futuristic look of wall-to-wall computers with blinking lights and beeps. In the technological world of space adventure viewers expect operating-room cleanliness, push-button control of communication, and robots that are as intelligent, if not more so, than people.

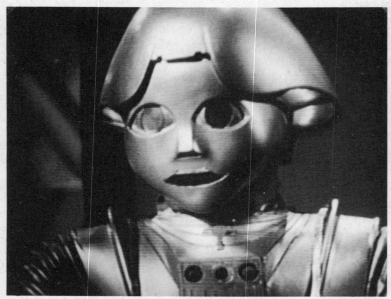

A futuristic robot companion assists Buck Rogers in his 25th-century space adventures

But the space people, although assisted by robots, still act like some of the traditional American heroes. Buck Rogers, like the old Western hero Buck Jones, is often dressed in white. His sleek, tight-fitting space suit shows off a handsome body, and he engages the bad guys in judolike conflict, knocking them over railings and saving the heroines. The heroines, dressed in interstellar style, have none of the cumbersome attire of the astronauts and are consistently good-looking. Hand in hand these new-age men and women work, like Captain

Video and earlier Western heroes, to overcome the forces of evil and to maintain order.

Some of television's heroes and heroines stay on earth and show how human beings, like machines, can and will be updated and improved by technological genius. These men and women gain unusual powers following a severe accident. In putting them back together, advanced medical and electronic techniques not only restore their normal powers but also provide superhuman skills. The "bionic" men and women and "incredible hulks" of the 1970s transcended the limits of time, space, and causality and used their powers to fight ordinary and extraordinary villains.

Early in 1980, *Beyond Westworld* gave a slightly different twist to bionic creaturehood. The series extended some of the motifs of the movie *Westworld*, in which sophisticated scientists and technicians produced robots so humanlike that they could become playmates for people who wanted to act out their fantasies in other times, places, and environments. One could, for example, vacation in the old West with lifelike robots who were indistinguishable from ordinary human beings.

The television series featured the struggle between a mad scientist, Quaid, and a security agent, John Moore. Quaid, not wanting these extraordinary machines to be used simply for entertainment, put the robots to work to gain power for himself. At the opening of the series an ad in *TV Guide* summarized the major motif in a question: "How do you kill a man . . . who's a machine?"[20] From the back seat of his automobile the power-mad scientist monitored the action of his humanoid robots. The "anatomy" of these machines was almost invulnerable; one had to hit just the right spot in order to destroy them. While Quaid manipulated these robots for his own demonic purposes, Moore and his companions worked desperately to identify and destroy them, which they did each week. Quaid was left to make diabolical use of the other machines in the next episode.

In shows like *Beyond Westworld*, the viewer gains a certain anticipation of progress in technology and a confidence that human beings will ultimately use it responsibly. Whenever human inventiveness is corrupted, the villains are presented as irrational, maniacal, power-hungry individuals who use technology for their own evil ends. Ultimately, reasonable, well-intentioned men and women can usually win out over these villains and redirect technology for the good of humanity. The "new," "better," "more improved" aspects of technology harmonize with the programs. Whatever can be invented should be invented. Little doubt is cast on the vision of individual or community life dominated by science and technology. Nor is there much questioning of the wisdom and will of most human beings to use the vast array of inventions for the good of all. Like commercials, most science fiction programs follow a simplistic rhythm of problem and solution.

While science fiction programs have provided many popular images of technology, the most enduring symbols of the technological society have come not from fiction but from actual broadcasts of space exploration. In the late 1950s and 1960s, the televised space ship launchings provided public images that activated national pride and gave viewers a sense of belonging to a great technological order. Those who saw the launchings still recall the excitement and drama of the last few moments of the countdown, the anticipation of the unknown and unpredictable, the grandeur of the energy that could send the space ships and their occupants soaring into the mysterious regions of the cosmos. As communication became more sophisticated, viewers on earth saw the occupants of the craft go about their daily activities in space.

It has already been suggested that views of the earth relayed through television from outer space could evoke in the viewer a sense of awe that might inspire thoughts of our ultimate origin and destiny. More obvious, and perhaps more commonplace, was the evocation of the sense of technological power and monumental human achievement. One value that could readily be identified from the images of the space missions was that of a responsible technology. These images gave visible evidence of progress and new possibilities for human life hitherto described only in fiction. We saw images "live from the moon" and heard the voice of the astronaut as he lowered himself onto the moon's surface. Television transformed the human heroism and scientific success of those memorable, fleeting moments into public, symbolic records for all citizens to witness.

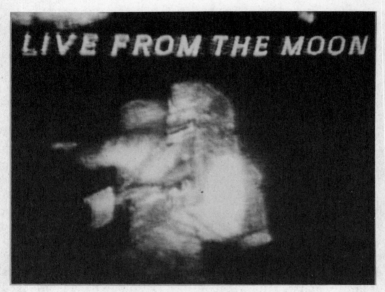

When the U.S. put a man on the moon, television transformed scientific success into a symbolic public record

In recalling those moments it is important to remember that political and economic institutions have always been conscious of symbolism. One comparison that comes to mind is the building of the Parthenon in fifth-century Athens. In the years after the defeat of the Persians, Athens was the most powerful and influential Greek city-state. What better way to celebrate and underscore that position than to construct a magnificent temple. No matter how much disorder was manifested at that time, citizens could see tangible evidence of Athens' grandeur embodied in the Parthenon.

It is perhaps symptomatic of our own times and culture that no ordinary cultural form — architecture, painting, or sculpture — has rivaled the space missions in their symbolic authority. The missions made the supremacy of technology visible to the nation and to the world. The astonishing space images — printed and telecast — were the most significant American secular icons for the generation after World War II. Not until the unleashing of space-age weaponry on the primitive agricultural society of Vietnam did many find these symbols a bit jaded.

The icons of technology — those of both fiction and fact — make visible a world sustained by faith in science and human inventiveness. The heroes and heroines of technology are men and women who combine reason, strength, intelligence, and a superb command of mathematics and electronics. Many of the questions raised by the imaginary and real adventures in space are still being explored.

In the beginning of this chapter, the traditional religious icon was introduced as a model for understanding how television images present us with symbolic universes in which we locate ourselves and our beliefs. Yet none of the American secular icons are further removed from traditional ones than those symbolizing science and technology. More than images of family and nature, the icons of technology have challenged the world, models, and questions of traditional sacred images. The heroes and heroines in the sacred icons were portrayed as exceptional human beings, although morally frail; their images witnessed a faith in divine, transcendent being. The icons of technology, by contrast, celebrate a faith in science and in human inventiveness. They proclaim a gospel that can deliver persons from ugliness, age, even death and destruction. Central to the new faith is the belief that human nature is not constant and that people, like products, can continually be changed, updated, improved, and packaged.

The icon, secular or religious, identifies an institutional order to which we belong, whether our belief in it is passionate or tenuous. Churches, nations, political parties, and corporations use images and other forms of communication to inspire confidence and channel loyalty. In our pluralistic society there are diverse institutional powers; we are simultaneously members of many communities and relate to many icons. The secular icons, however, tend to push aside or absorb the older religious ones. There are still traditional images on the walls of museums and churches, but secular icons in the print and electronic media saturate our environment. Their very pervasiveness often screens us from traditional sacred images. Inescapably present, secular icons dominate the sphere of public symbols.

III
Iconoclasm:
Images on the
Attack

The term *iconoclasm* comes from the Greek words *eikon*, or "image," and *klao*, "to break." The iconoclast is one who breaks images. In the ancient world it was common in many religious traditions to associate the live presence of the god with the image itself. Images, especially sculptural forms, manifested the presence and being of the deity. The power and personality of the god were not confined to the image, however. The god was conceived as active in the world as well. The effigy was not only a tangible form by which a person could honor and please the god, it was also a means through which the deity could bestow benefits on mortals. As Edwyn Bevan comments, attitudes toward these images ranged widely in the ancient world:

> Between the belief of the peasant, who took the ani-
> mation of the idol in its most gross realistic sense,
> and the belief of the educated man, who regarded the
> ceremonies of worship as only expressing in a sym-
> bolic way that there was some unseen power some-
> where, who liked to receive the homage of men,

there may have been any number of intermediate shades.[1]

Because of the power attributed to the image, defacing or smashing it meant destruction of the deity, or at least of one particular manifestation. When one tribe or nation conquered another, it was important to destroy the images of the local god.

In the Jewish tradition the worship of images was ridiculed and condemned. Worship should be directed only to the transcendent God. Iconoclasm was part of the priestly and prophetic traditions that constantly denounced the worship of images. Thus the destroyer of images was one who guarded against the tendency of persons to conceive of the holy in human form and to worship such forms. The ancient Hebrews were not the only ones to have this attitude. Xenophanes, the early Greek philosopher, thought it inappropriate for the gods to appear in the guise of animals or human beings. But in the Hebrew tradition this admonition against the making of images was codified in the second of the Ten Commandments.[2]

Christianity, arising out of Judaism, inherited the iconoclastic attitude toward images. Gradually, however, the Christians developed their own interpretations, as evidenced in Roman Catholicism and Eastern Orthodoxy. During the Protestant Reformation the iconoclastic position was strengthened and out of this reformed tradition a variety of attitudes emerged, from complete prohibition of images to their use in the portrayal of Bible stories.[3]

In the nineteenth and twentieth centuries, iconoclasm has referred to an attitude, rather than to the physical act of smashing an image. The iconoclast is a person who attacks established beliefs or institutional authority through words or images. Printing first opened up new ways to undermine social, political, and religious authorities when adversaries used pamphlets, magazines, and newspapers to persuade people of the falseness or injustice of particular systems. With improved printing processes, the case of the iconoclasts was strengthened, as they could then "document" the injustices with pictures. Film extended the power of the iconoclast in a different way; moving sights and sounds could be organized into an argument against the establishment. Today, we are just beginning to understand some of the ways in which television contributes to the transformation of iconoclasm. Paradoxically, in this sophisticated world it is not the destruction but the production of images that may best accomplish the aim of iconoclasm, the elimination of false powers.

Iconoclasm Before Television

Printed Images

Using images to deface and undermine prevailing powers certainly did not begin with modern mass media. The etchings of Goya in his *Disasters of War* series and the masterful lithographs of Daumier in the mid-nineteenth century were models of draftsmanship and effective political satire. In this country, Thomas Nast made many Americans aware of the power of the image to criticize political and religious authorities. His cartoons played an important part in the downfall of Boss Tweed and the corrupt Tammany Hall in the late nineteenth century. Later, Tweed escaped from jail and fled the country. It was through one of Nast's images that he was recognized, captured, and returned to the United States. Nast, however, did not restrict his images to criticism of politicians. His work reflected an anti-Catholicism that may have lingered in the national attitude toward public figures until the election of John F. Kennedy. One of Nast's cartoons showed an obese pope surrounded by his attendants atop the dome of St. Peter's, with a telescope pointed in the direction of the United States. The caption read: "The Promised Land, as Seen from the Dome of St. Peter's, Rome."[4]

The Masses magazine (1911–1917) became the center of iconoclastic activity for many American artists and writers in the early twentieth century. Institutional positions under attack in today's world were also fought out visually in this magazine. Pacificism, women's rights, racism, birth control, abortion, militarism, and big business were all there. Artists like John Sloan, Stuart Davis, and George Bellows were major contributors. There was a remarkable satirization of big business by John Sloan in which he drew a great, immobile, grotesque human hulk. A minuscule man on its back held a lance, which, when compared with the size of the enormous creature, was like a tiny pin. The giant human hulk was identified by the initials "N.A.M." and the ineffective little person wielding the pinlike lance was identified as "investigation." The caption: "National Association of Manufacturers: If that keeps on itching back there, I'll have to scratch."[5] Artists and writers combined their efforts to attack major economic and political establishments, but the magazine had only a small circulation; most of its readers were intellectuals like the artists and writers who ran the magazine. *The Masses* came to an end with America's entry into the First World War. Artists on its staff, like Boardman Robinson and Art Young, later became leading political satirists for newspapers across the country.

The effectiveness of iconoclastic images was closely related to the techniques of printing and dissemination. Goya was an etcher and the impact of his work depended upon the circulation of prints. Daumier's lithographs were drawn on sensitized stones from which editorial caricatures were printed in newspapers and magazines. Nast's drawings were made into engravings and printed as illustrations in *Harper's Weekly.* Photography, however, offered a new technique for documenting evidence.

Photography became a major tool for the social critic in the late nineteenth and early twentieth centuries. Two outstanding photographers were Jacob Riis and Lewis Hine. Riis, arriving in New York from Scandinavia in the 1870s, suffered the plight of many immigrants in tenements of New York. When he finally got work as a police reporter, he verbally criticized the system and environment that allowed this human degradation. Later, he took with him a photographer to illustrate the conditions he was describing, and still later, he himself began to photograph. His pictures pointed out more forcefully than words the abuses and neglect within the social system.

Lewis Hine, a man of similar sensibilities, later criticized the same system. Speaking to a social work conference in 1909, Hine said:

> Whether it be a painting or photograph, the picture is a symbol that brings one immediately into close touch with reality . . . In fact, it is often more effective than the reality would have been, because, in the picture, the non-essential and conflicting interests have been eliminated.[6]

Hine came to New York in 1901 in order to study at Columbia University. Arriving from Wisconsin, he had looked forward to studying and understanding the city. Like Riis, he became thoroughly disenchanted and turned to photography to dramatize the fate of the poor and homeless arriving in this country. His portraits of Ellis Island immigrants presented the viewer with questions about the society these immigrants were entering. Through his photographs he vigorously attacked the manufacturers who employed children for long hours and low wages. These photographs endure through the decades as some of the most poignant, stark judgments ever made against the exploitation of individuals for institutional profit. A small boy stands rigidly, self-consciously, as his picture is taken against the background of a machine that he must watch and tend. Hine's caption: "Leo, 48 inches high, 8 years old, picks up bobbins at 15 cents a day. Fayetteville, Tennessee. November, 1910."[7] Hine worked as investigative cameraman for the National Child Labor Committee and traveled all across the country. His work is a classic example of modern iconoclasm: images that incriminate unjust powers and exhort viewers to change the system.

Hine has sometimes been called the originator of the documentary school of photography in this country. But the term *documentary* is misleading. As William Stott points out in his *Documentary Expression and Thirties America*, the term *document* in the sense of an impersonal, objective record exists only in legal documents or precise historical records that furnish evidence or information. Most of the images we call "documentary" are the opposite of this kind of official evidence. The human document "carries and communicates feeling, the raw material of drama"[8] and is derived essentially from the human condition. All persons understand such documents because of common human experiences — birth, marriage, death, suffering, work. Stott's book focuses primarily on the "social documentary." His concept can be directly related to the iconoclastic image:

> Social documentary . . . shows [people] at grips with conditions neither permanent nor necessary, conditions of a certain time and place: racial discrimination, police brutality, unemployment, The Depression, the planned environment of the TVA, pollution, terrorism.[9]

These images are designed to evoke an awareness of social, economic, or political problems that are subject to change. Thus when Hine and Riis are referred to as "documentary" photographers it is in the sense of social documentary or iconoclastic. The word Hine himself used was *interpretive*. The social reality was interpreted by the photographer and that interpretation was laden with the photographer's own sense of condemnation.

In the early twentieth century Hine represented the image-maker as fierce iconoclast. He was not simply interested in aesthetics but was equally motivated by ethical concerns. Hine's photographs are indeed powerful in their aesthetic construction, and their beauty fortifies their assault upon conscience. But exhortation, not aestheticism, was his driving passion. The purpose of the iconoclastic photograph was to shatter the system that permitted the injustice.

This prophetic role in the tradition of Hine and Riis was

carried out in the thirties by other photographers, among them Dorothea Lange and Ben Shahn. Working for the Farm Security Administration they shared the iconoclastic views of Hine and documented the plight of the disinherited farmers and migrant workers. Dorothea Lange first worked as a fashionable portrait photographer. Later, she closed her studio and began to photograph the victims of the Depression. Working first with Paul Taylor and later for the Farm Security Administration, she dramatized in her photographs the weary and worried faces, the desperate circumstances of homeless, workless people on the move. Her photograph entitled *Migrant Mother* has meaning beyond the thirties and is just as effective today as a symbol of the poor. Like Hine, Dorothea Lange kept notes on her work and these witness to her involvement with her subjects:

> In a squatter camp at the edge of the pea fields. The crop froze this year and the family is destitute. On this morning they had sold the tires from their car to pay for food. She is thirty-two years old.[10]

Similarly Ben Shahn's work represented the prophetic impulse of the iconoclast. Using photography, painting, and graphics, Shahn was able to express his social concerns and protests in a variety of ways. After a series of paintings in the late 1920s protesting the sentencing of Sacco and Vanzetti, he continued to use painting for judgmental images as well as for integrative images of community life. His photographs of the thirties, like those of Lange, provided a sharp contrast to the illustrations of Norman Rockwell on the covers of the *Saturday Evening Post*. Shahn's images of a tenant shack — patterns of weathered boards, rusting nails, broken and reflecting windowpanes — show Shahn, the artist, achieving beautifully unified compositions. But, gazing through the window, the partially hidden faces of a mother and child reveal Shahn, the social critic, who was concerned with the plight of the poor. Shahn was remarkable among American artists for the breadth of his work and for his ability to describe the artists' roles. In his book *The Shape of Content*, he wrote about the pursuit of truth as a basis for criticizing values.

> The beliefs in what constitutes truth change with every generation, with each new great preacher or teacher or cataclysmic discovery or a deep revelation through art or music or drama or poetry. Whatever our momentary concept of it may be, it seems as though truth itself is that objective which awakens the purest passion . . . It is in pursuit of truth perhaps that we are able to sacrifice present values and move on to new ones. And I am sure that it is most often in the light of what we believe to be truth that we criticize negatively or reject the values of others.[11]

The spirited conscience that motivated the work of these and other artists of the thirties continues to animate contemporary iconoclasts. The photographer W. Eugene Smith, for example, has enabled us to see the enormous range of human heroism and madness in war. From Saipan, in 1944, he wrote about his war photographs.

> . . . and each time I pressed the shutter release it was a shouted condemnation hurled with the hope that the pictures might survive through the years, with the hope that they might echo through the minds of men in the future — causing them caution and remembrance and realization.[12]

As a maker of icons, he photographed Albert Schweitzer in his African mission. But it was the prophetic iconoclast who went to Japan to photograph the victims and indict the industry that had poisoned and disfigured a village's people. The photos in Smith's *Minamata*, published in 1975, show the same moral outrage that characterized his earlier work.

Documentary Film

Improvements in photography and printing processes allowed images to circulate among larger and larger audiences. A quantum leap came when moving pictures arrived. This was to be one of the most influential techniques for iconoclastic imagemaking. The moving image offered the iconoclast a medium that combined sight and sound. The communication of values was made more effective by shifting the camera focus, editing, and extending the time during which the viewer's attention was sustained.

In the 1930s independent film makers and persons in governmental agencies recognized that film held new possibilities for mediating social values and for consolidating public opinion. In Germany, more so than in the United States, leaders understood film as an instrument for communicating political ideology. During the Roosevelt administration, efforts were made to use the medium for public communication about government policies. Two such films, *The Plow That Broke the Plains* (1936) and *The River* (1937), dramatized some recently enacted policies. In these films the new techniques helped visualize the abuses of a socioeconomic system that had led to the devastation and impoverishment of agricultural areas and other natural resources. Written and directed by Pare Lorentz, with music by Virgil Thomson, the combination of sights and sounds beautifully dramatized the historical circumstances of the economic crises and the depletion of environmental resources. The first parts of both films are iconoclastic, showing the failure of socioeconomic policies to assure continued productivity and wise land use. The judgmental aspects of the films made the viewer aware of the problems in previous land use policies. Once the critical statement had been made, the films ended on a positive note, showing what the Roosevelt administration had accomplished.

In other countries experiments in the use of film to call attention to social ills were already underway by the mid-1930s. John Grierson and Paul Rotha, from England, argued most vig-

orously for films that could evoke political awareness. Both
men saw the power of film to alter social and political attitudes. For Rotha the documentary film could and should be at
the cutting edge of communal thought.

> Your documentarist creates documentary and be-
> lieves in the documentary method of cinema because
> he considers it the most powerful means of social
> expression available today.
>   Yet, despite my plea that the maker of docu-
> mentary should be politically and socially conscious
> in his approach to everyday experience, he has no
> claim to the label of politician. His job is not upon a
> platform to harangue the mob but in a pulpit to per-
> suade the mass to a wider consideration of human
> affairs. He is neither a fighter nor a barnstormer.
> Rather is he a prophet concerned with the broadest
> references of human associations. He is a propagan-
> dist making use of the most influential instrument of
> his time. He does not march with the crowd but goes
> just ahead, asking contemplation and discussion be-
> fore action is taken on those problems with which he
> deals.[13]

Rotha wrote those words in 1935. *The Plow That Broke the
Plains* and *The River* were to be produced a few years later. But
it was in Germany that the iconic and iconoclastic power of
the documentary tradition was best understood in the 1930s.
Under the direction of Leni Riefenstahl, colossal productions
were filmed to spread the ideas of the Nazi party.

With America's entry into World War II, film in the double
role of iconifier and iconoclast helped enlist and unify soldiers
and civilians and identify the enemy. One of the films in the
Why We Fight series produced by Frank Capra was *War Comes
to America*. It detailed events leading to America's entry into
the war. Through animation, clips from newsreels and old
films, it gave a visual interpretation of the actions taken by foreign powers and the changing American attitudes toward the

world conflict. The dramatic climax came with the surprise attack of the Japanese on Pearl Harbor at the moment that their ambassadors were in Washington on a mission of peace. The iconoclastic facets of the film depict the aggressive acts of Germany and Italy and, ultimately, the treachery of the Japanese. At the same time the iconic elements helped the viewer become aware of belonging to a greater, just cause. This was achieved, in part, by depicting "average" citizens as they responded to the events and world pressures between 1931 and 1941. The force of the film was its dramatization of the changing attitudes of Americans during those years and their total involvement with the war effort by the end of the decade. Toward the end of the film this solidarity was expressed by superimposed images: a waving United States flag overlaid with images of G.I.'s marching, one by one, into confrontation with the enemy.

The films in the *Why We Fight* series were designed primarily for those who were being indoctrinated by the military, although many were seen by civilians and some translated into other languages and shown abroad. During World War II all of the nations at war used films both to identify the enemy and its unrighteous cause and to envision the nation and its just cause. The war underscored both the iconoclastic and iconic force of film. Erik Barnouw, film and TV historian, characterizes the documentary production thoughout World War II as "the bugle-call film, adjunct to military action, weapon of war."

> The film maker's task: as to the faithful, to stir the
> blood, building determination to the highest pitch; as
> to the enemy, to chill the marrow, paralyzing the
> will to resist.[14]

Because of documentaries and newsreels there arose a new kind of civilian enlistment and participation in national life. But the steady fare of images also continued through photographs and illustrations in weekly magazines, such as *Life*. On these pages, the images of war — allies and enemies — were distilled for readers to contemplate. Movie theaters and magazines brought a weekly rhythm of images. And every day the words of overseas correspondents shaped radio and newspaper reports.

Iconoclastic Television

Television Documentaries

One of the great iconoclasts of American television, Edward R. Murrow, served as a radio correspondent during World War II. Through the imagination and voice of Murrow broadcasting from London, Americans could visualize in their minds the heroes, attackers, and the struggles to the death. After the war, in 1951, Murrow worked with Fred Friendly to develop a series entitled *See It Now.* As a result of telecasts dealing with Senator Joseph McCarthy and McCarthyism, the program became a prototype of iconoclastic television. As Erik Barnouw has observed, their program was launched just at the time that the older film series, *The March of Time,* was dying out.[15] That series, which had started in 1935, played in movie theaters, using a documentary format. Unlike most newsreels, *The March of Time* attempted to get at issues, rather than give brief, summarized news coverage. With *See It Now* Murrow and Friendly were bringing that investigative journalism into television. But it was two years before *See It Now* tackled the issue of McCarthyism. They were, in fact, criticized for not examining this issue sooner. But, as Barnouw aptly phrases it, "The Murrow Moment" came, and late in 1953 the confrontation between McCarthy and Murrow began to take shape.

When Murrow learned that Lieutenant Milo Radulovich, a meteorologist in the air force Reserve and a student at the University of Michigan, had been asked to resign his commission, he sent a staff member to get more information. The lieutenant's sister and father had been accused of being political radicals, though their accusers had not been identified. Radulovich refused to resign his commission. But, on the grounds of security, an air force board at Selfridge Field had ordered his separation. Murrow and his team investigated the incident; they were able to get many filmed interviews from the Radulovich family but none from the air force. Although the network and others exerted pressure on Murrow to drop it, the show was produced. Barnouw's description of the final moments suggests the excitement and tension over the program:

> All were aware that Murrow was not merely probing the judicial processes of the air force and Pentagon — a quixotic venture few broadcasters would have undertaken at this time — but was examining the whole syndrome of McCarthyism with its secret denunciations and guilt by association. They were also aware that the disease was not peculiar to government but had virulently infected the broadcasting industry — including CBS.[16]

The program went on the air and Murrow concluded it by offering the air force an opportunity to comment on and correct any of the information. He then added:

> Whatever happens in this whole area of the relationship between the individual and the state, we will do ourselves; it cannot be blamed upon Malenkov, Mao Tse-tung or even our allies. It seems to us — that is, to Fred Friendly and myself — that it is a subject that should be argued about endlessly.[17]

The program gave Murrow, in Barnouw's words, "a momentum that would now not let him go." This and Murrow's subsequent programs dealing directly with McCarthy gave to TV iconoclasts a model of courage in political investigation and reporting.

On March 9, 1954, *See It Now* focused directly on McCarthy. The program had been designed so that it relied primarily upon images of McCarthy himself; if it damaged him, it was largely because the senator had done most of the talking.

Again, Murrow concluded with only a brief, but penetrating comment:

> The actions of the junior Senator from Wisconsin have caused alarm and dismay amongst our allies abroad and given considerable comfort to our enemies, and whose fault is that? Not really his. He didn't create this situation of fear; he merely exploited it, and rather successfully. Cassius was right: "The fault, dear Brutus, is not in our stars but in ourselves. . ." Good night, and good luck.[18]

Just as Murrow had offered time to the air force to reply to his program, he offered McCarthy a chance to respond. McCarthy did take the opportunity to do so, using the program to attack Murrow. Telecast on April 6, 1954, it was another occasion for viewers all over the nation to see McCarthy's tactics, another opportunity to observe, to hear, and to form judgments.

Americans had learned to trust Murrow's calm voice on the radio during the war years. In *See It Now*, the calm voice was coupled with his lean face and searching eyes. His telecast portrait was strikingly dissimilar to McCarthy's portrait and body language. Murrow's image was philosophical, low-key, nonjudgmental: "The fault, dear Brutus, is not in our stars, but in ourselves." The portrait of McCarthy was aggressive and accusatory. Speaking of Murrow on *See It Now* in 1954, McCarthy described him as "a symbol, the leader of the cleverest of the jackal pack which is always found at the throat of anyone who dares to expose individual communists and traitors."[19]

For some Americans, Senator Joseph McCarthy from Wisconsin was a cultural hero who was "telling off" subversives and making sure they were identified and punished. For others, he was a satanic figure. To all persons, television in its early years proved to be an effective iconoclastic instrument against political authorities who abused their powers.

In choosing what can best be placed before viewers, the television iconoclast must reckon with the size of the home TV screen. The moving images and sounds of television must

Edward R. Murrow, a model of courage in political investigation and reporting during the McCarthy era

be reduced in scale to fit this small frame. Therefore, TV investigative journalists make emphatic use of portraiture. The size of the screen in the home gives the viewer in the ordinary tight shot a one-to-one relationship with the person being televised. Moreover, the camera can move in so that the screen is filled with magnified portions of the subject's face, such as the eyes and forehead. Just as the human eye records the features of another's face, the television camera can scan a face from different angles. It may cut quickly from face to hands, showing fists tightly clenched or fingers nervously tapping. Pulling away slightly, the camera can include posturing and gesturing.

In *See It Now* and in subsequent investigative television, body language and portraiture have been basic to viewers' judgments about the character of persons and the institutions they represent. McCarthy was the first major politician on which the judgmental power of the new medium was tested. Ironically, iconoclastic television gives to politicians a unique opportunity to self-destruct through their own images.

In addition to programs like *See It Now*, the television documentary continued to bring to the American public profiles of its political leaders and of the government's foreign and domestic policies. In the 1960s, documentaries on all three networks presented some of the disturbing aspects of national policies. NBC produced a series of specials called *NBC White Paper*, the first of which was about the so-called spy plane, "The U-2 Affair." From the ABC-TV series *Close-Up* came "The Children Were Watching." At a time when integration was about to be given a new impetus through the election of John F. Kennedy, this documentary about a small child attending the first integrated school in New Orleans demonstrated the adversary role that television could play.

The CBS *Harvest of Shame* was telecast the day after Thanksgiving, November 25, 1960. The choice of the time was itself significant; pictures of the rootless migrant workers clashed with those of Macy's Thanksgiving Day parade. *Harvest of Shame* brought an old problem back into focus; the visual motifs were similar to those used by Ben Shahn, Dorothea Lange, and the photographers of the Farm Security Administration during the Depression. The medium had changed but the human situation was the same: temporary camps, persons out of work, open trucks stuffed and overflowing with persons desperate to get some kind of work in the fields and orchards. Some of the earlier still photographs could have been interchanged with particular frames in the television documentary. It was as though those earlier portraits of people and their environments had suddenly assumed life and motion. The new dimensions of motion and time added psychological impact to the visual symbolization of people on the move, ever in search of a harvest. Interspersed with portraits of the workers, their families, and surroundings were images of truck wheels in motion. These close-ups of the ever-turning wheels carrying human migratory creatures from site to site heightened the viewer's sense of these workers' instability and rootlessness.

The iconoclastic imagemaker's intent is to exhort people to take action, to change the system in a way that will reduce injustice. But it is not at all clear that legislation has radically altered the fate of migrant workers. A single documentary is not likely to do more than sensitize serious viewers to conditions under which some persons live in this society. On the other hand, when the documentary comes as a climax to a larger, broader effort to communicate some of the abuses and dangers of established practices, it can work in a catalytic way. The documentary *Silent Spring* investigated the problem of pesticides and their danger to the environment. It was an especially interesting example of the use of portraiture to dramatize the conflict between environmental, ethical, and economic issues. There were many close-up shots of the author, Rachel Carson, whose earlier book *The Sea Around Us* had sensitized the public to the problem. Video images of her face communicated serenity and poise, yet great passion — portraits of a caring woman showing righteous indignation. The images of the spokesman for pesticides — thick, dark-rimmed spectacles dominating an asymmetrical, graceless, thinly mustached face — seemed almost comic in comparison to the elegant and poignant portrayal of Rachel Carson.

In addition to portraiture, the documentary showed vividly how the environment was affected by pesticides. It is one thing to read about, but another, more emotional experience, to see devastation and death in nature. Iconoclastic television was especially powerful when, on the screen before the viewer, a robin writhed in convulsive spasms; it was difficult for a nature lover to be dispassionate. These images, along with the books and other forms of public discussion about the problem, mounted a formidable opposition to the indiscriminate use of pesticides. Shortly after the program, Congress enacted legislation limiting the use of pesticides that were harmful to the environment.

The actual effects of iconoclastic documentaries are difficult to ascertain. *The Selling of the Pentagon*, aired by CBS on February 23, 1971, evoked considerable discussion. Written and produced by Peter Davis and narrated by Roger Mudd, its subject was the close relationship between the Pentagon and business contractors. It also showed the Pentagon's efforts at propaganda through public demonstrations of weaponry. Public reaction to the program included both praise and hostility. Jack Gould, writing in the *New York Times* on March 7 of the same year, called it a "magnificent blow for progress" in "hard hitting reporting that was impeccable in its integrity, absorbing in its revelations and a priceless guideline for electronic journalism." He commended it for its departure from "wishy-washy coverage" of Washington and for its "independence of government manipulation of the news."[20] The *Times* reported on March 21 that Vice President Spiro Agnew denounced the program as "a clever propaganda attempt to discredit the defense establishment of the United States." He further accused the network of putting together military officers' remarks out of context "to create a false impression" and of obtaining under false pretenses interviews with important public figures.

But what about the actual impact of this documentary on public attitudes? Political scientist Michael J. Robinson, using data from the Survey Research Center at the University of Michigan, calculated the results of experiments with three groups that had been shown *The Selling of the Pentagon*. The first group saw only the documentary itself. The other two saw the documentary followed by a videotape discussion. The second group saw a twelve-minute videotape in which F. Edward Hebert, Chairman of the House Armed Services Committee, Vice President Agnew, and Richard Salant, then president of CBS News, set forth their opinions about the program. The third group of subjects saw a tape in which the remarks of Hebert, Agnew, and Salant had been paraphrased. Robinson found that those subjects who saw only the documentary, without any additional discussion, had changed their ideas about governmental misconduct. The documentary "moved some portion of our middle Americans toward holding an image of the armed services that was more sinister and misbehaving."

> Group A subjects perceived the military as: more
> likely to lie about the War in Vietnam, more likely
> to get involved in politics and more likely to seek
> special political advantage than these subjects had
> previously believed.[21]

Robinson's data showed that in the other two groups the effectiveness of the documentary was diminished by the subsequent videotape. An important further finding was that, for all the groups tested, the program raised doubts about their own ability to cope with or understand politics.

> In short, the program frustrated viewers, regardless of
> mode of presentation. And a close reading of the data
> suggests that subjects, in every mode, were at least
> as willing to doubt their own capacity to compre-
> hend politics as they were to question the legitimacy
> of the institutions involved.[22]

Robinson went on to suggest that people who depend on TV for their political information might exhibit "videomalaise," a cynicism and sense of impotence about participation in political life.

Whether or not dependence on TV for news and political information leads to cynicism and pessimism about institutions, a curious fact is that in 1979–1980 *60 Minutes* had one of the highest Nielsen ratings of any program. If the Nielsen measures are correct, many Americans tune in regularly to this kind of investigative journalism. On the basis of the popularity of this show it could be said that people are highly entertained if not instructed by the weekly exposure of institutions, groups, or individuals who appear to be violating public trust. Of course, not all of the reports on *60 Minutes* are anti-institutional or antiheroic; they also feature poignant and heroic individuals who are coping with life in an extraordinary way. One program dealt with a network of communication and support among young children who are dying of cancer. But more typical are stories investigating modern-day Nazism, industrial pollution, and political corruption.

The *60 Minutes* logo has become for many Americans a symbol of iconoclastic journalism

Programs that are intentionally or unintentionally iconoclastic may lead to cynicism about institutions. Or, in combination with other information sources they may produce inertia. In Ernest Becker's words, we may be "choking" on truth.[23] The staggering superabundance of information — in newspapers, magazines, books, radio, television, billboards, direct mailing, handouts on the street — contributes to an informational overload on the human mind. One result may be a short-circuiting of our ability to act, or worse, a loss of confidence in our ability to affect any of the modern principalities and powers, whether it be the Pentagon or multinational corporations.

Harsh judgments about human behavior existed long before television. What may be different in modern communications is our response to them. We cling to a confidence that we can make choices, but the channels for action seem narrow. Our frustration may be in part that we are saturated with information, global in magnitude, yet our existential field of action remains, as it always has been, quite limited.

Inadvertent Iconoclasm

Whether drawn, painted, printed, or televised, iconoclastic images have dominated the work of many American artists who have deliberately used images to question and criticize social, economic, and political institutions and the persons who represent them. Their prime target has been the abuse of authority, and their images have been designed to deface or destroy unjust policies. There is, however, in television an inadvertent iconoclasm, where images are not intentionally critical, but become, in fact, adversary images.

Some inadvertent iconoclasm originates in television coverage of important political inquiries that are opened up to the public and the media. This kind of iconoclasm can be traced back to the early history of television. Shortly after the *See It Now* programs on McCarthyism Congress held hearings to investigate the dispute between McCarthy and the army. They began in April 1954 and ABC-TV network carried them in their entirety.

Unlike the *See It Now* programs, which were deliberately designed and edited, the continuous coverage of the hearings on McCarthy's dispute with the army had no such editorial design. The cameras simply rolled on, allowing the viewers to perceive the issues as they unfolded. Most important, they allowed the viewers sustained portraits of the actions and gestures of the persons involved in the dispute. Murrow's programs had given television viewers two episodes in which Joe

McCarthy's gestures, facial expression, and voice became known. The continuous coverage of the hearings extended the portrait and spread it before a larger public. The image of McCarthy was accompanied by those of his aides, especially Roy Cohn. In the hearings, Attorney Joseph Welch communicated a character quite different from that of McCarthy; his wit and dignity did much to discredit the senator from Wisconsin. The televised hearings were a visualization of conflicting personas. By the end of the year McCarthy was condemned by his Senate colleagues. Before then, television viewers had already judged him. The result of the prolonged exposure was an inadvertent iconoclasm on the part of the medium.

Twenty years later, the president of the United States, Richard M. Nixon, was judged through similar televised hearings. The investigative journalism of Woodward and Bernstein of the *Washington Post* had drawn national attention to the Watergate break-in and the possible involvement of persons close to the president. But Nixon did not testify as McCarthy had. Instead, his aides appeared for hours before the cameras in the committee hearings. Carried on both public and commercial television, with the three major networks rotating coverage, the hearings became a public spectacle. While some stations received calls from viewers complaining about the preempting of their favorite programs, many people found new daytime entertainment. Barnouw has pointed out that the Watergate hearings won rating battles for the networks:

> Watergate became an obsession with viewers. Some
> watched live hearings all day, the taped repeats at
> night. Chairman Sam Ervin, with his store of Bible
> quotations and aphorisms, became a folk hero. The
> long, detailed testimony of former White House
> counsel John Dean — extremely damaging to the
> President — riveted the national attention.[24]

Part of the fascination of the Watergate hearings was the interrogation that was done, not by the committee, but by cameras that hovered over both the witnesses and the committee members. Following formal legal procedures, the senators, one by one, put questions to the witnesses. But the cameras constantly scanned and probed, ruthlessly and unrelentingly. On Tuesday, June 26, 1973, the day after John Dean's first testimony, the *New York Times* carried a three-column photo of Dean under this large headline:

DEAN TELLS INQUIRY THAT NIXON TOOK PART
IN WATERGATE COVER-UP FOR EIGHT MONTHS
HE ALSO NAMES HALDEMAN AND EHRLICHMAN

But neither a newspaper photo nor a transcript of his testimony could equal the damaging effect of the portrait of Dean that had appeared on television on that first day of his testimony. Viewers saw the entire frame of their screens filled with his face. Sometimes the camera moved in with a tight shot in

In the Watergate hearings, cameras as well as senators interrogated witnesses like John Dean

which every motion of his eyes could be followed. Cameras monitored every expression that might assist or damage his credibility as a witness. In the political drama being enacted, John Dean's persona symbolized doubt and distrust of the president.

No one escaped the interrogation of the cameras. They roamed freely about the hearing room and with zoom lenses could pick up Mrs. Dean's expression as she responded to one of Sam Ervin's folksy remarks. Viewers could almost become a part of the huddle between witness and lawyer. Cameras supplied the TV audience with every scandalous remark that slipped from the lips of the actors. No wonder the hearings were doing so well in the ratings.

The technical sophistication of camera work went far beyond that of the Army-McCarthy hearings. Viewers could peer over the chairman's shoulder at documents that witnesses were asked to explain. In one instance the crew-cut, blue-eyed Haldeman was asked to identify a letter describing plans for hecklers to disrupt a Billy Graham rally and shout obscenities. In the left margin the word *good* had been handwritten and the word *obscene* was underlined in the text of the letter. The camera moved from the document to the clean-cut countenance of Haldeman to Chairman Sam Ervin's face, capturing his amazement and incredulity. Laughter, shuffling, the sights and sounds of spectators' movements reinforced moment by moment the viewer's own reactions. Obviously, any member of Congress who saw the televised Watergate hearings would be doubly cautious about the use of television in broadcasting the proceedings of Congress itself. As it has turned out, the cameras there are kept in tight rein. There is no free play of cameras on audience or respondents.

I have used the phrase "inadvertent iconoclasm" to describe both the telecast hearings of the Army-McCarthy dispute and those associated with the Watergate episode. In both instances the hearings were not isolated, but were part of a larger process of investigative journalism that preceded the telecasts. People all over the country had, to some degree, been exposed to the issues and personalities involved; the public had been sensitized through the media of print and radio.

The reporting of controversial issues in print offers a great deal that television cannot. One has a chance to reflect, go back for a second reading, or compare one report on an issue with another written from a different point of view. Television coverage is a very different kind of reporting, especially when cameras are brought into spaces where public hearings or investigations are under way. There is really no way to predict how witnesses or interrogators will appear before the cameras. It is in this sense that the word *inadvertent* is used; the cameras are there simply to record an event. Images take on their iconic or iconoclastic tone through the utterances, demeanor, and faces of those who participate in the event. Some of the interrogators in the Watergate hearings, for example, gained unusual national visibility. The televised images of the hearings also became inadvertently iconic. Few persons had heard of Sam Ervin before these hearings. Yet, for several years after they were over, his portrait lived on in American Express commercials. Thus some politicians emerged as heroic, whereas others were seen as demonic.

Instant, incessant portraiture through television can easily be misleading. Many of the appearances and utterances that are captured on the screen may be accidental and out of context, often encouraging viewers to make quick, superficial judgments about political personalities. Television has become such an important part of political portraiture that the visual image becomes a basis for substantive judgments. It is no wonder that politicians are concerned about their good looks.

In the television era, public officials can never escape the presence of the camera. President Truman, who was not under constant video surveillance, had a somewhat better chance to create his own public image than many of his successors. The new power of television to create icons or to destroy them was most memorably exemplified in the Kennedy-Nixon debates of 1960. Kennedy's image emerged from those debates as a new kind of political portrait, created and styled by television.

Later presidents, realizing the importance of video portraits, have appropriated the techniques of public relations and advertising early in their campaigns. Agencies handle campaigns and promote politicians as they promote products. And once the president is elected, the office brings undreamed-of resources for developing political portraits — news conferences, telecasts of important speeches and of meetings with world and national leaders, filmed reports of tours, and so forth. In a discussion of the adversary role of the press, Bill Moyers commented:

> It means that the President can announce a position
> and a policy before an audience of millions without
> fear of rebuttal. It means that a lie or a distortion or
> a deception can pass into the public consciousness
> without the dissenters or the people who can say
> that wasn't so, having the same forum. And it puts
> in the hands of a skillful performer an enormous
> power to bypass the small audiences that read indi-
> vidual newspapers.[25]

With the increased power of imagemaking, there is no guarantee against the creation of false images. But in a free society the inadvertent iconoclasm of television may function as a balance to the massive imagemaking capability available to those in the highest governmental office.

The News

All networks — public and commercial — participated in some way in the broadcasts of the Watergate hearings. This situation differed markedly from the more ambiguous attitudes of the networks in 1966 when the Senate Foreign Relations Committee scheduled hearings on the Vietnam policy. Fred Friendly resigned from CBS because it had decided at first not to carry the hearings. In his letter of resignation, Friendly criticized the network for making a mockery of the news division's crusade to gain access to congressional debate:

> We cannot, in our public utterances, demand such

access and then, in one of the crucial debates of our time, abdicate that responsibility.[26]

Under criticism, CBS resumed coverage of the hearings.

In the beginning, opposition to the Vietnam War was muted and cautious. Eventually the day-to-day ritualistic news coverage began to deface the political and military policies in Vietnam. In 1963 the networks increased the time for news from 15 minutes to half an hour. In the later sixties these newscasts were filled with reports of dissent and protest and, as the war escalated, the nightly news programs were dominated by scenes of violence and suffering. Television was moving toward a role of adversary or iconoclast within the ritualistic format of the news.

In the early years of the war in Vietnam representatives of the press and television seemed to embrace the patriotic spirit and style of coverage that had been established in World War II. But as the war grew in length and became more controversial, the correspondents and photographers changed their style. The war itself was quite different from others this country had fought. Eventually the images sent back and presented on the evening news programs had an iconoclastic effect. Rather than consolidating patriotic sentiments about our involvement, the images began to erode public support of the war effort and to confirm other forms of criticism of our military role. Certainly no war had ever been made so graphic, and these intensely visual, khaki-colored, blood-bathed, defoliated images gave concrete symbols to the dissent in this country. They transmitted into living rooms the raw, brutal suffering of soldiers and civilians alike; citizens watching the daily news programs could not avoid these grim reports. A young marine was seen undergoing surgery. The screen was filled with close-ups of his face, and occasional shots of tubes and plasma, as surgeons tried to save his leg. One of the attendants lit a cigar and put it in the patient's mouth. As the operation took place, his grimaces and attempts to smile added an intensely personal dimension to the reporting. Our sympathies went out to civilians as well.

Children running from napalm bombs did little to enlist our loyalty to the war. In less violent frames, tanks and war machines were juxtaposed against a background of peasants harvesting crops.

In the course of the war, the news reporters in Vietnam became some of the leading iconoclasts. On March 28, 1974, WNET produced a program entitled *The Adversaries*, which looked back at the role that the press had played in American history. In reflecting upon the Vietnam coverage, it showed that the war had been covered by a new generation of American journalists whose roots were in the protests and marches of the 1960s, not in World War II. Brendan Gill, in that program, remarked that it was a generation which, "with a vision of the world shaped at Selma and Little Rock, developed a hard-eyed skepticism of the establishment. They were the ones who first went to report the war in Vietnam, while their elder colleagues remained behind to pace the corridors of power in Washington."[27] Morley Safer was not one of the young reporters whose roots were in the 1960s, but it was his report, the famous "Zippo" story, that shocked many Americans. Safer's reflections to Brendan Gill are instructive:

> MORLEY SAFER: The old rules of reporting the war were quite simple. You took a press handout, say — I'm exaggerating — you actually went in the field with the troops. Well, the identification between the trooper and the reporter was very close, I mean, you were on his side, the enemy was wrong... Those rules were probably quite valid in the Second World War and perhaps even in Korea. But there was something very smelly about Vietnam that everyone was aware of and nobody wanted to talk about.

> GILL: Morley Safer's 1965 film report showing American Marines setting fire to peasant huts with Zippo lighters stunned millions who saw it on national television. Adversary reporting had begun its resurgence.

SAFER: The Zippo story probably cut more deeply. I think it was an extraordinary shock to a lot of people, as they sat there watching the Cronkite news and seeing American troops shoving old men and old women along with their rifles, and burning down thatched cottages. Well, it happened.[28]

The adversary role of television in Vietnam was an obvious example of deliberate iconoclasm that was at first inadvertent. Placed in the ritualistic context of the regular news programs, these reports had an added impact because of the repeated, rhythmic sequences. Night after night images of death and destruction came upon the screen. Soon many Americans, not just college students and reporters, were questioning our involvement in Vietnam.

The credibility of the networks and their interpretations of the news figure prominently in what is called here "inadvertent iconoclasm." What the reporter is *saying* can inform the viewer of the state of affairs of past, present, or future situations. As E. H. Gombrich has pointed out,

Language performs this miraculous function largely through such little particles as "if," "when," "not," "therefore," "all" and "some," which have been called logical words because they account for the ability of language to formulate logical inferences.[29]

Images, by contrast, are supreme in their capacity to evoke emotions and arouse sentiments. What they lack in precision of tenses they more than make up for in their capacity for arousal. In the television frame there are often images behind the reporter to which viewers respond. A typical news report from Washington, for example, will not show simply a talking head but the reporter filmed against the background of the Capitol or the White House. We attend his or her words on one level; meanwhile the portrait of the reporter and the symbols in the background are shaping our impressions of the spoken words.

The images and their ability to communicate are intensified when commentators are speaking but are not seen on camera. When just the voice accompanies the moving sights and
sounds of an event, there is less an impression of interpretation
and more a sense of "telling it like it is." Take, for example,
some of the images that dominated the evening news programs
while American reporters were in Teheran covering the take-
over at the American Embassy. Regardless of what the voice of
the reporter was saying, the images of the Iranians — clenched
fists, flags, posters, jeering crowds — were operating on the
emotions of the viewer. International conflict, or the appearance of conflict, was mediated via satellite into everyone's
home. These iconoclastic images, which identified the
"enemy," increased Carter's popularity for a short time.

Interpretation and authenticity are intimately connected
in the photographic image. While a photograph assumes a part-
nership between the real world and the image machine that
takes the picture, most persons neglect to consider the third
partner, the photographer. It is this third partner who gives the
decisive interpretation to any photograph. The first step in the
interpretive process is selection of a subject. From that proceed
many more: isolation of the subject, camera angles, lights,
cropping, and so on. The selective process becomes even more
complex in television. Yet, the sense of "reality" grows. The
moving images and sounds of the war in Vietnam, for example,
heightened the viewer's sense of authenticity.

Viewers need to understand that news images are interpretations. All newsworthy items — a political candidate's visit to
a particular city, natural disasters, guerrilla warfare, diplo-
matic disputes — have undergone many stages of interpretive
selection before the images fill up the screen on the evening
news. Viewers do not respond to events; they respond to symbolic records of events.

Comedy

It would be a mistake to think that iconoclasm in television occurs only in the news and documentary formats. Adversary positions toward political and social institutions have appeared in the songs, parodies, impersonations, and melodramas of television comedies. Scholar and critic David Thorburn has pointed out that entertainers were among the first to voice the unrest of the 1960s, anticipating the political caricatures of the 1970s. Their wit also softened up and prepared audiences for more straightforward and aggressive investigative journalism in the late 1960s and early 1970s.[30] To the mime and clowning of a Lucille Ball or a Red Skelton the later comedians added pungent satire, passion, and political relevance. They addressed controversial issues with biting humor, invoking impiety through laughter and bringing a new vigor into TV iconoclasm.

Tom and Dick Smothers burst out of the boundaries of social satire into politically sensitive issues. The Smothers Brothers brought into their *Comedy Hour* politically unacceptable persons and ideas. At a time when protests against the war in Vietnam were receiving only occasional news coverage, they invited the blacklisted Pete Seeger to sing his Vietnam protest song, "Knee Deep in the Big Muddy," on their show. This comic team entertained Americans with hard-hitting, irreverent humor that attacked respectable institutions — religious and political. Attuned to college students, these programs appealed particularly to youths who were themselves involved in protest but who had had little access to a public platform. A few years later, *Rowan & Martin's Laugh-In* capitalized on the new mood of satire that was very popular in the late 1960s. Not only its satire but also its innovative techniques found immediate popularity. Reaching much larger audiences than the usual documentary, this show focused a glaring spotlight on political issues and personalities. Comedians, along with investigative journalists, took on the Pentagon and politicians.

The style, pace, and bruising satire of these earlier comedies gave way to more unusual format in NBC's *Saturday Night Live*. Simulated newscasts and satiric commercials bristled with caricatures of political leaders and corporate institutions. Chevy Chase poked fun at Gerald Ford as a bumbling, stumbling, head-bumping president. Dan Ackroyd caricatured Jimmy Carter's grin and mimicked his ingratiating Southern manner. While the satire was sometimes gross, it was fearless in its choice of victims.

Shortly after the accident at Three Mile Island, *Saturday Night Live* presented a bizarre, vitriolic parody, calling attention to the dangers of radiation. "Jimmy" and "Rosalynn" Carter paid an official visit to Two Mile Island, where a Pepsi spilled in the control room had triggered a nuclear disaster. After a conference with plant officials just outside the contaminated room, a confident and smiling "Jimmy" in large yellow insulated boots courageously entered the dangerous area to investigate and put public fears to rest. Meanwhile, the others waited outside paying no attention to the cleaning woman who shuffled routinely about her work. She, too, disappeared into the contaminated room. As "Rosalynn" and the plant officials continued to chat among themselves, there slowly loomed outside the window the gargantuan toothy smiling face of the "president." His enlarged features took up half the space of the window frame. Next to him, the grotesquely large head of the cleaning woman slowly rose into view. While "Rosalynn" and the officials looked on with horror, the mutated couple turned and smiled at each other, cheek to cheek.

Election years offer repeated opportunities for political satire; these entertainments, like the news programs, follow the candidates, issues, and events from caucuses to conventions to elections. The formats have been generally the same — irreverent melodramas, spiced by ridiculous impersonations of vulnerable public figures. Trivializing and distorting as they are, these programs continue, or breathe new life into, the spirit of Thomas Nast's biting satire.

Resistance to Iconoclasm

Some critics contend that serious television does not get

tough enough with the economic and political establishments or with itself as a power. Why is this so?

Some would argue that there are restrictions on documentaries because of production problems. Neil Hickey, writing on television and investigative reporting, comments on the logistical problems that hamper the best efforts of undercover reporters. He quotes the writer and producer of *The Selling of the Pentagon*, Peter Davis:

> If Woodward and Bernstein had shown up at their
> rendezvous with Deep Throat lugging a camera,
> lights and sound equipment, the whole Watergate
> exposé might never have happened. People who want
> to remain anonymous simply are not going to have
> their pictures taken, even in disguise.[31]

Furthermore, great expenditures of time and money are required to do the hour-long broadcasts that explore controversial subjects. Critic John Culhane claimed in a *New York Times* article that there were "seven deadly taboos" in television documentaries — big labor, big business, big TV networks, the automotive industry, nuclear power, the military-industrial complex, and U.S. foreign policy.[32] Later, in a letter to the editor of the *Times*, John Sharnik, vice president of CBS Public Affairs Broadcasts, pointed out the exceptions to those taboos and added:

> The only taboo around here is the professional's hor-
> ror of lousy journalism...A documentary often con-
> sumes as much of a journalist's life as it would take
> him to write a book: several months, sometimes a
> year. No producer worth his weight in out-takes
> wants to undertake a commitment like that unless
> he believes he'll come out with something worth an
> hour of the viewer's time.[33]

Since that exchange between Culhane and Sharnik, national and international crises have determined the agenda of documentaries. The event at Three Mile Island, for example, clearly weakened any taboo about discussions of nuclear power. Unexpected events undo restrictions set by production costs or networks and create public pressures for more adequate news coverage and investigative journalism.

Under the present system of broadcasting, advertisers sponsor most programs. This places unfortunate restrictions on journalists. It is hard to conceive of a steady flow of programs in which sponsors see some of their own hallowed values and economic interests scrutinized by investigative reporters. Moreover, Culhane in his criticism of network documentaries claimed that the network executives don't seriously consider proposals for subjects that have not won good ratings in the past.

> They know that such programs would not interest sponsors more interested in profits than prestige — a category that includes the vast majority of sponsors — and they fear that tough-minded, controversial reports would scare off even those few high-minded sponsors who, despite their desire to do good, are not interested in tarring themselves with a brush likely to offend a good many viewers.[34]

Thus the accusation of timidity and caution in iconoclastic documentaries assumes a circular motion from network to sponsor to viewers and back to network.

Are the viewers themselves, the television public, the final arbiters of what goes on in hard-hitting documentaries? Do the viewers (the ratings) determine the selection of controversial and noncontroversial subjects? Under the present technological and economic system it seems reasonable to expect that they do. Large communications systems, whether they be governments, businesses, or industries, do not want to displease viewers, especially in a democratic society where votes or sales of products are at stake. Paradoxically, it is the action of some individuals and networks, in the face of all the limitations, that sometimes brings iconoclasm into television. The classic case mentioned earlier was the Murrow-Friendly decision to focus on McCarthyism. The two men paid for an advertisement themselves when they could not get support from the management. And it was ABC that alone among the networks dared to survey world opinion on the war by broadcasting *The Agony of Vietnam* in 1965. This came one year before the hearings of the Senate Foreign Relations Committee on Vietnam policy.

But a real eye-opener about the limits of iconoclasm came on September 5, 1977, when *The Guns of Autumn*, produced by Irv Drasmin, was telecast. This documentary did not investigate the cataclysmic rumblings of nuclear plants, delicate foreign policy, or the cosmic power of multinationals. But it hit a raw nerve in American society. The subject was not arcane or taboo. Most ordinary Americans were very familiar, in one way or another, with the subject. Everybody knows somebody who is a hunter, and guns can be bought almost anywhere. The documentary focused on what is, for some, a regular fall event, for others, a big business, and for still others, something basically lamentable. The film might be compared to *Silent Spring* insofar as it argued for conservation of wildlife. But the pesticides that Carson attacked in the earlier documentary were harmful, at least indirectly, to human life as well as to wildlife and the environment. In *The Guns of Autumn* the hunters seemed boorish in contrast to the helpless animals that were shot. The treeing and shooting of a bear seemed particularly brutish and senseless. So inflamed were the sensibilities of both anti-hunters and hunters that the documentary drew more mail and phone calls than any documentary in CBS history.

The documentary was indeed so controversial that there was a follow-up program by George Murray, *Echoes of "The Guns of Autumn,"* narrated by Charles Collingwood. It came as no surprise to hear that hunting enthusiasts and, of course, the gun lobby had been outraged and had vehemently criticized the network for the documentary. It was, however, shocking to learn of the financial pressures that had been exercised. Almost all commerical sponsors had withdrawn their support of the documentary before it was telecast. Collingwood reported:

> We had hoped to film interviews on this whole subject of commercials with the sponsors, advertising agencies and CBS sales executives involved. They all declined.[35]

Those who saw the program will remember that public service announcements dominated the spaces where commercials were supposed to be. Collingwood explained in detail that

> on Tuesday, September 2nd, "The Guns of Autumn" was previewed by stations affiliated with the CBS Television Network. That's normal practice. . . . In the days following that preview, eight previously scheduled commercials were dropped from "The Guns of Autumn." The sponsors pulled out in some cases after telephone calls from pro-hunting organizations. For example, Combe Chemical Company had scheduled three 30-second commercials for Lanacane, Grecian Formula and Odor-Eaters. Its advertising agency canceled those commercials as the result of a call from Norden Van Horne, director of the Denver branch of Safari Club International. He said the program misrepresented hunting in the United States and was unsuitable for home viewing. . . Whatever the reasons, the sponsors who canceled included Aqua-Tech, Lenox Air-Conditioning, Williams Lectric Shave, Datsun and Mr. Coffee.[36]

Obviously this was not a popular documentary. But genuinely prophetic criticism is by nature unpopular. In this system censorship can easily operate against controversy by withdrawal of financial support. Collingwood told viewers that only one commercial sponsor had remained with the documentary — Block Drugs. Although the company had received several calls from Thomas Hodges, director of public affairs for the National Rifle Association, "it felt cancellation of its commercials would mean it was trying to censor a major news medium, and that, it said, would be contrary to fundamental American tradition."[37]

Ironically, it was another "fundamental American tradition" — hunting — that had come under scrutiny; the iconoclasts were smashing idols. Therefore one should not be surprised by the uproar *The Guns of Autumn* produced. If the documentary were rerun today, it would probably engender the same response as in 1977. Contemporary idol smashers should remember that the "false gods" they attack are very real "gods" indeed, and the assault against sacred images is not taken lightly. Prophets have been stoned.

IV
TV: A
Substitute for
Sacraments

The analogical use of ritual and icon in the interpretation of television depends fundamentally upon a broad definition of religion. It acknowledges a common thrust for life and meaning that transcends the usual distinction between "secular" and "religious." A football game, a political convention, and a Christian mass are vastly different, but they all register the organic thrust to survive and to survive with meaning. From a sociological perspective, religion is essentially a "symbolic universe," a social product that provides an overarching framework, ordering and interpreting human experience. Peter L. Berger and Thomas Luckmann assert that this nomic function "puts everything in its right place."[1] The symbolic universe helps people to make sense of both individual and social experience. Biographical events — birth, marriage, death, sickness — are understood through institutionalized patterns of interpretation.

In primitive societies the rites of passage represent this nomic function in pristine form. The periodization of biography is symbolized at each stage with reference to the totality of human meanings. To be a child, to be an adolescent, to be an adult, and so forth — each of these biographical phases is legitimated as a mode of being in the symbolic universe.[2]

But, as these scholars point out, it would be a mistake to think only of primitive societies. Modern society can also offer myths and symbols that help one to "know who one is."

But there is more to the phenomenon of religion than the creation of symbolic universes that order the rhythms of life. Religion is a manifestation of the awesome and holy, of transcendent being. Peter Berger, sociologist of religion, goes beyond the idea of religion as a human construct to discover "signals of transcendence." He identifies them as essential qualities of human experience that point beyond "natural" reality — the human propensities for order, for play, hope, moral outrage, and humor.[3]

Religion also concerns itself with faith. In his introductory essay to *Radical Monotheism and Western Culture*, theologian H. Richard Niebuhr describes faith as "the attitude and action of confidence in and fidelity to certain realities as the sources of value and the objects of loyalty."[4] Expressed in praise or confessed in a creed, faith is a trust that gives value to the self and at the same time to that which the self values. To this confirming aspect of faith Niebuhr adds its counterpart, the active side of faith as expressed in loyalty or commitment to a cause. It is in this dual sense that Niebuhr understands faith in the political community and in science as well as faith in gods, goddesses, and God. Nationalism provides an example of a "center of values" in the culture.

> When the patriotic nationalist says "I was born to die for my country" he is exhibiting the double relation that we now call faith. The national life is for him the reality whence his own life derives its worth....His life has meaning because it is part of that context, like a word in a sentence. It has value because it fits into a valuable whole...But faith in

the nation is primarily reliance upon it as an enduring value-center. Insofar as the nation is the last value-center to which the nationalist refers, he does not raise the question about its goodness to him or about its rightness or wrongness.[5]

The community of the nation or the family, the natural order, and the "world" of science and technology may all be centers for human confidence and loyalty. It is the ability of cultural orders to evoke faith in the sense of both trust and loyalty that makes the analogy between religious and secular symbolic forms appropriate. The secular icons are mediators through which people can strengthen their identification with these centers of value. Furthermore, Niebuhr asserts that when God is the object of ultimate trust and loyalty, all other things are sacralized. This conclusion not only encourages analogies between sacred and secular forms of communication, it opens the possibility of a religious critique of cultural forms and a cultural critique of religious forms.

If H. Richard Niebuhr describes the human propensity for faith and loyalty to secular institutions, Ernest Becker adds a basic human need for play and illusion.[6] In his book *The Denial of Death*, Becker asks: "On what level of illusion does one live?"

[A human being] needs a "second" world, a world of humanly created meaning, a new reality that [one] can live, dramatize, nourish [oneself] in. "Illusion" means creative play at its highest level. Cultural illusion is a necessary ideology of self-justification, a heroic dimension that is life itself to the symbolic animal.[7]

To lose the security of heroic illusion reduces persons to a kind of animal level, Becker believes, and he speaks of the loss in modern life of heroic, convincing dramas.

If there are no ready-made traditional world views into which to fit oneself with dependency and trust,

religion becomes a very personal matter — so personal that faith itself seems neurotic, like a private
fantasy and a decision taken out of weakness. The
one thing modern [men and women] cannot do is
what Kierkegaard prescribed: the lonely leap into
faith, the naive personal trust in some kind of tran-
scendental support for one's life. This support is now
independent of living external rituals and customs:
the church and the community do not exist, or do
not carry much conviction. This situation is what
helps make faith fantastic. In order for something to
seem true . . . it has to be supported in some way —
lived, external, compelling. [Human beings] need
pageants, crowds, panoplies, special days marked by
calendars — an objective focus for obsessions, something to give form and body to internal fantasy,
something external to yield oneself to.[8]

This suggests that ritual and icon, which supply occasions for
creative play and fantasy, are concrete forms transcending any
particular epoch or religious tradition. More than that, it
seems possible that the modern emphasis on the rational and
the banishment of illusion and mystery has left a vacuum to be
filled by other, secular forms. As we have seen, visual images
play an important role in shaping our perceptions. It may be
that some of the power of television is that, in providing precisely those pageants, panoplies, and special days, it gives an
"objective focus for obsessions."

Ritual Revisited

Television coverage of the inaugural mass of Pope John Paul II
was described in Chapter I as an extension of ritual experience.
The televised world travels of the pope in 1979 provided further
examples of how the medium could reach millions of persons.
The visits were covered in great detail, especially his trips to
Poland and to the United States, and the new pope (the first

Vicar of Christ to appear on the cover of *TV Guide*) became known to believers and nonbelievers alike. His warmth and openness endeared him to many who had no relationship to him other than that of friendly spectators trying to catch a glimpse of a celebrity.

Wherever the pope went, he celebrated the mass. Let us consider, for example, the mass performed on the Boston Common the first evening the pope visited this country. The Common had been elaborately prepared for the occasion; major local stations carried the telecast. During the mass pouring rain fell upon the faithful and even burst through the protective canopy over the celebrants. Commentators inevitably spoke about the torrential drenching as well as the events and processes of the mass. Actually, the weather dramatized what physical presence means in ritual experience. Ritual participation is not primarily a matter of watching, but of acting and being engaged with the sights, sounds, and smells of the spiritual event. Television, however, narrows the range of sensation to seeing and hearing. The faithful believer who watched the chalice being offered and heard the words of the celebrant could not taste the ritual wine. The Eucharist that evening, with soaked Christians sloshing up to receive communion, while priests held umbrellas over the pontiff, was a vivid reminder of the importance of physical presence in Catholic ritual.

Although attendance at the mass on Boston Common was limited, television gathered millions into the liturgy. The reverent viewer felt at one with the crowds at the event and even sensed a feeling of grace as the pope extended his blessings over the airways. Some viewers even phoned television stations to be reassured that blessings received through their TV screens were authentic. In spite of all its limitations, TV ritual did, in the Niebuhrian sense, locate people's centers of value and sources of self-value. These images had the capacity to show aspects of the "whole" of which viewers were a part.

The analogy between TV and traditional forms is most effective when participation means observation or simply shar-

ing one's joy or sorrow. The inauguration of a president, for example, is a national celebration. The selected persons who
have special seats and can watch the event from close range
enjoy the spatial ambiance of this event. But for TV viewers,
television extends the ritual elements. TV images generate
faith in the nation and its institutions. Patriotism is stirred by
multiple scenes — the Washington Monument, close-ups of
the president and his family, dramatic views of the flag flying
over the Capitol dome or of the monumental statue of Lincoln.

Similarly, the funeral of John F. Kennedy, an occasion for
sharing the national loss of a president, allowed mourners to
locate themselves in a larger whole. That funeral was perhaps
the prototypical ritual event of television. Physical presence
was secondary to catching sight of the flag-draped coffin being
lowered down the steps of the Capitol, sitting before the
images in bewildered grief as others had stood for hours, and
seeing the riderless horse and caisson drawn to Arlington
National Cemetery. Indeed, for events such as the inauguration and the mourning for a national hero, television becomes
essential to the event. Where sentiments are deeply felt, television is not simply an extension of ritual but an integral part
of it, dramatically bringing into consciousness those centers of
value that give significance and worth to individual selves.

The analogical use of ritual to understand television is
strained when applied to news programs. The nightly news
does more than simply give the news. It structures a visual and
verbal mosaic of events. Its camera techniques resemble those
used on election night, but it offers a regularly repeated pattern, meeting expectations with familiar sounds and faces, in
the same order, at the same time, and on the same channel,
night after night. Perhaps *ritualistic* is a more appropriate term
to indicate the attempt to dramatize, to introduce rhythms and
interpretive patterns into news reporting. In a society that has
tended to de-emphasize the sacramental, it may be that ritualization of even the most nonsacred events is a response to a rit-
ually deprived population. Just as traditional rituals offered
opportunities for relating the self to a transcendent order, in a

secularized society a regular event like the nightly news can answer a need for ritual.

To be sure, even if there are ritualistic aspects in the news, most newspersons would claim that this is *not* the function of the news media — print or electronic. Reporters and editors see their roles, rather, as persons who responsibly, and as objectively as possible, report events that are worthy of public attention and reflection. Kenneth Briggs, religion editor for the *New York Times*, has emphasized that newspapers, magazines, and television are not intended to make up for the lack of ritual or collective feelings in this culture. A ritualistic relationship to the news might be cultivated by readers or viewers, but the development of this relationship is clearly not the intent of print or electronic newspersons.[9] Robert Northshield, executive producer of CBS's *Sunday Morning*, noted that in a similar way persons tend to ascribe iconoclastic or adversary roles to television news reporting. With some exceptions, the iconoclastic motifs in television news programs are inadvertent, rather than deliberate.[10] Even though we all agree that the primary purpose of a responsible press is to inform, there is, nevertheless, a tendency of readers and viewers to find in the news media a world view, and, in the television medium, a ritualistic form of communicating that sense of the whole.[11]

At the heart of ritual experience are what Ernest Becker refers to as the "twin ontological motives": the longing to be a part of a greater whole and at the same time to stand out as a separate individual.[12] In a mass, for example, both of these motives are held in balance. There is the individual action of the believer who eats the bread and drinks the wine, and there is the absorption of the self into a larger frame of reference. When individuality is subverted, however, the passion to be part of the whole can become an occasion for tyranny. Watching Leni Riefenstahl's 1934 film *Triumph of the Will*, for example, is a shocking experience in that it captures just such a drive to lose one's own identity and merge with a greater cause. Some of its sequences are satanically majestic in presenting

the image of Hitler against a human sea of thousands of obe-
dient, faithful troops.

Today we are subject to different, more subtle subversions
of ritual and individuality. The media ritualization of politics,
news, sports, and public events has both positive and negative
consequences. For those who have little or no access to
"pageants, crowds, panoplies, special days," television supplies
a sense of belonging to a larger whole, a center of value that at-
tracts and molds the individual. The darker side of electronic
ritualization is its tendency to inspire and market conformity.
The danger lies in losing oneself to such a degree that the capacity of individuals to stand out as something separate and
unique is destroyed.

Icon Revisited

In traditional Christian icons there were distinctive characteristics not found in modern images. The sources of the
church's iconography, for example, were usually sacred scrip-
tures and mythology. In Eastern Orthodoxy the differences
were even greater. There the form and fabrication of the images
were determined by strict formulae, the sanctity of the images
resulting from the manner and circumstances in which they
were made. Moreover, in both Eastern and Western Catholic
traditions icons were generally meant to be contemplated in
special places — shrines, churches or other sacred sites.

It is obvious that images on television match none of these
characteristics. Occasionally Biblical stories are dramatized —
Zeffirelli's *Jesus of Nazareth* was broadcast on commercial television — but most TV shows draw their subjects from secular
culture. There are no comparable static formulae or fixed traditions: style and technology are constantly changing. Nor are
there special contexts: TV sets are everywhere — in bus stations, restaurants, bars, homes, and schools. Nevertheless,
despite these differences, both the traditional and the electronic icons render visible the invisible centers of meaning
and value.

> It is a curious and inescapable fact about our
> lives. . . that we cannot live without a cause, without
> some object of devotion, some center of worth,
> something on which we rely for our meaning.[13]

Faith as loyalty to a cause or center of worth is an important
element in the creation of images. Even secular images glori-
fy some god, advance some cause or symbolize some "world."
The old and new icons work in similar ways — offering models
of human behavior and determining what questions are to be
asked.

For many persons in a secular society the older sacred
images have been put aside, objects relegated to museums. At
the same time, their presence lingers and they are unique because of the special worlds, models, and questions they stand
for. The central questions of the old icons were those of human
suffering, death, and redemption. The figures portrayed were
models of human behavior because they had learned to live by
God's grace and pointed the way for others. The "world," which
gave ultimate significance to human experience, included not
just the present world, but looked back to the beginning and
forward into the beyond. The presence of an infinite being extended the framework in which finite human destiny, both
individual and collective, was acted out. The symbolization of
that world defied ordinary perceptions of time and space and
offered possibilities for a cosmic heroism.

Today the traditional icons are no longer popular, and they
may never be again. The models to follow and the questions to
pursue are a burden, unwanted by most and difficult to bear for
the few who have chosen them. Big Mac and Coca-Cola have
become substitutes for more demanding sacraments. Yet,
while the old icons have less general acceptance, they may,
even in a secular society, play a normative role. They keep
choices open and offer standards by which people can evaluate
contemporary icons.

Heroes and heroines in the secularized iconic world of television bear little or no resemblance to traditional Christian

saints and martyrs. Yet a residual element of the heroic model
is present. Writing for *TV Guide*, the late Margaret Mead
called attention to what many people already suspected:

> TV more than any other medium gives models to the
> American people — models for life as it is, or should,
> or can be lived. New styles spread faster, and they
> have more reality for people if they are shown on
> TV.[14]

Contemporary secular heroes have their place in a long contin-
uum of extraordinary persons who have become objects of
veneration. A small boy speaking of his World Series hero commented to a reporter, "He's like me!" The hero offers a magical
likeness and evidence that certain accomplishments are really
possible. However idealized, falsified, or glamorized, models
furnish examples for others. As the movies offered heroic
images in the 1920s and '30s, TV furnished role models in the
late twentieth century.

The quality of the models that appear on the television
screen is constantly under assessment. In its study *Window
Dressing on the Set: Women and Minorities in Television*, the
United States Commission on Civil Rights reported that the
television world of the 1970s presented a social structure in
which men were very much in control of their lives and in a
position to control the lives of others. Females, in contrast,
were younger, family bound and often unemployed. Those
who worked were seen in stereotyped and sometimes subservient occupations. Women were also more often portrayed in
comic roles. Men were shown as authoritative figures with in-
ordinate physical and mental strength.

> The infallible lawyer, the authoritative chief of po-
> lice, the invincible detective, along with countless
> subordinates, uphold the law and maintain order on
> television. While these images are pervasive in ac-
> tion-adventure shows, another facet of the strong
> masculine character is revealed in the omniscience

and self-righteousness of the doctors, teachers, and fathers who solve the myriad problems which arise in television's melodramas. In contrast, the limited number of roles for women, the lack of depth with which they are portrayed, and the degree to which they are dependent on males for their sustenance, security, and safety in the face of psychological and physical threats have formed the basis for much of the criticism of television's depiction of women.[15]

The report also criticized television's depiction of minorities. It pointed out that there were relatively few roles for them and those that did exist were token ones or contributed to stereotyped images.

In an article in *Ebony* magazine, Jack Slater has written about the problem of stereotyping blacks. Slater noted that a decade ago black males, if they appeared at all, were "emotionless, ultra-cool, one-dimensional figures" in dramatic series such as *Mission: Impossible.* In 1979 three series challenged the stereotypical images of black males: *Paris*, portrayed by James Earl Jones; *Benson*, starring Robert Guillaume; and *The Lazarus Syndrome*, featuring Louis Gossett, Jr. Today, however, black men are still seen principally as "one-dimensional comedy figures — loud-mouthed buffoons, precocious brats and finger poppin bucks passing as Black males in such sitcoms as *Good Times*, *The Jeffersons* and *Different Strokes.*" Slater expresses pessimism about any significant changes in the image of the black male in prime-time television since whites are primarily responsible for the writing, directing, and producing of these shows:

To that degree, television's new primetime Black man is depressingly similar to the old one in that he, too, is a creation of Whites. "One of the penalties of being Black and having limited money is that we seldom control our own image," Black actress Ellen Holly once wrote in a newspaper article. "We seldom appear in media as who *we* say we are, but rather, as who *Whites* say we are."[16]

In the conclusion to its 1977 report, the commission took note of this phenomenon. It related some of the stereotyping to the networks' pursuit of higher ratings and higher profits.

> Stereotyped portrayals of minorities and women, which have been part and parcel of successful program formats, are perpetuated by the networks in their pursuit of higher ratings and higher profits. The surest route to a highly successful and highly profitable program schedule is to create new series based on formats that have already proven popular. Old formats are used until they eventually fail as advertising vehicles. Moreover, network programmers are afraid of offending the sensibilities — whether real or imagined — of large segments of the viewing public.
> Programming designed to reach the widest possible audience, coupled with the demands of the ratings race, constrains writers and producers from introducing more realistic and diverse images of women and minorities to the television screen. Thus, network programmers with one eye on successful old formulas, the other on the inoffensive, and both hands in their pockets are not oriented toward serving public interest.[17]

In their 1979 update, the Civil Rights Commission concluded that in the late 1970s the stereotyping had not changed and, indeed, in some cases, had intensified.[18]

Super-Icon: The TV Commercial

Disdained though it may be, the TV commercial is the most distinctive icon in our secular culture. Almost all products and human services, from an aspirin to the presidency of the United States, now depend upon TV advertising. Worthy and less worthy products and people are indiscriminately advertised if there is money enough to pay for ad agency services. The result is a unique technological sophistry under the direction of the promotional specialist, who, for a price, can enhance or tear down an image of a product or person.

The commercial works as a kind of "organic" connector — linking together consumers, imagemakers, producers, networks, sponsors, corporations, economic system — and contributes more to the mediating of ideas than any other type of programming. Since the subject of the commercial is the product itself, it can use any of the symbolic worlds that is most convenient. Although some ads work on the absurd and specialize in the comic and unlikely, the models are mostly "beautiful people." Through editing, fast camera changes, juxtaposition of jingles and images, the commercials enable these beautiful (or outlandish) people to state the problem and answer in a matter of seconds. Like traditional icons, commercials appeal to hope and fear. They even promise miracles. Their aim is to evoke in the viewer loyalty and conviction. Instead of fealty to king or savior, the fidelity is to products. "Faith," "loyalty," "trust," "confidence," "assurance," and, above all, "happiness" — all these concepts are woven in and out of the sights and sounds of commercials. The people are mostly like us, or as we would like to be. Blacks made it into commercials as the circle of heroic types widened to accommodate changing attitudes and a burgeoning market. By buying a product, everybody has a chance to become members incorporate in the mystical body of those who have been redeemed from obesity, ring-around-the-collar, bad breath, or simple human loneliness.

While the traditional icon was an image for contemplation, to be viewed with sustained devotion, the commercials whiz by in a matter of seconds, and many viewers simply tune them out. But the frequency with which they are repeated and the artistic skill with which they are designed make them linger in the consciousness. Consider the number of jingles from commercials that have been elevated to popular songs. The commercial has become a kind of visual, musical catechism that affects the way persons see themselves and the world.

It is possible that some of the success of contemporary advertising is due to its discovery and promotion of new public questions and resolutions, however trivial. Commercials, frothy as they are, may catch our attention because they cater to the human habit of raising questions and finding resolutions. Concern about body odor and the weekly wash could camouflage a need to ask more profound questions about mysterious and complex human experiences.[19] The endless, mindless questions and answers encountered in commercials are a fractured, sometimes pathetic witness to the persistenct human compulsion to raise questions and cope with life's processes. They also reflect the profound metamorphosis from Questions to questions, from the mysteries and miracles of traditional sacred truths to the mysteries and miracles of modern detergents. This transformation is accompanied by a metamorphosis of both images and faith: from gods to goods, from salvation to soaps.

While soliciting our loyalty in the purchase of particular products, advertising images simultaneously confirm citizenship in a larger economic-political order. They have become an indispensable part of our system of production and consumption. This country does not need to invest in a domestically oriented political art because, at the moment, that is provided by television commercials.

Jacques Ellul, a vociferous critic of technology, has developed a concept of "sociological propaganda."[20] In his view, political and economic systems are reinforced by cultural forms — advertising, film, television, education, and technology. He points out that few people view these as propaganda, but, in fact, these cultural forms slowly and gently condition people to a way of life that they consider as the only one, or the very best.

Furthermore, such propaganda becomes increasingly effective when those subjected to it accept its doctrines of what is *good or bad* (for example, the American Way of Life). There a whole society actually expresses itself through this propaganda by advertising its kind of life.[21]

In the United States this kind of propaganda became a means of unifying a population of immigrants who brought with them diverse traditions. It also played an economic role in the spreading of views "as to what the necessities of life [were]."[22]

Ellul's comments echo the words of other critics who attack television's materialistic values. Among them is Harry J. Skornia, who writes:

If television can be said to have any values at all, it is those of the salesmen, big businessmen, manufacturers and showmen who control it — essentially materialistic values. And, like those who control it, television shuns everything which does not fit with these values.[23]

If the traditional icon represented hope to the believing Christians and confirmed their faith, the secular icon of advertising dazzles the eyes of the faithful spender:

Television extols the spender. [The spender] is portrayed by the stars. . . buys everything. . . knows that it is a duty to free enterprise to spend, rather than to save. . . If children do not spend on mother, on Mother's Day, they obviously do not love her. Affection or loyalty, like success, is measured in dollars.[24]

A solid day of television viewing would fortify these statements. Though viewers may be unmoved by the commercials that parade across the screen, they will find it hard to escape thinking of themselves as consumers, members of a "Kleenex Culture" that promotes a use-and-throw-away consumption.

The source of the icons of the past was quite clear: the institutional powers of traditional religions. Who or what has the power to select the icons on television? The producers? The networks? Sponsors? The FCC? The ratings? Local stations? Technology itself? One thing seems clear: television is big business and represents big profits. It would be naive to think that this fact does not enter into the shaping of our myths, models, and questions. Skornia remarks:

> Farfetched as it may now seem, historians of the future may conclude that never before was there a period during which control of the thinking of a nation was exercised in a more totalitarian manner, or by a smaller group, than it is now by television and radio.[25]

It is also true, however, that when one leaves the border of a totalitarian country and returns to the open communication of a free society, even the superficial and innocuous slogans of commercials look good. They seem to suggest choice and freedom, however limited. Changes in federal legislation regarding communications and the media and, perhaps even more important, changes in technology will have an impact upon the concentration of power.[26]

Final Reflections

In discussing the iconic and iconoclastic motifs in television, I have made references to symbolic traditions in American art that have communicated public values. Since the late 1940s and 1950s, however, a major movement in American art has been aniconic, without images — nonrepresentational paintings, prints, and sculpture.[27] The critical success of this non-metaphoric, imageless aesthetic interrupted, at least temporarily, a visual tradition that has been predominantly iconic. This happened at the same time that television began to develop as a mass medium. There was a polarization of cultural forms. At one end of the spectrum were the nonobjective colors, shapes, lines of abstract expressionism, color field painting, and minimalist forms. At the other end were the incessant, lifelike images that began to flow across television screens.

While recognizable images presented viewers with concrete references to experience, imageless works provided no such common references. Consequently the nonrepresentational works raised a question for the general public that often seemed irrelevant to the artist and critic: "What does it mean?" In reviews of shows, and in essays and reflections upon these nonmetaphorical works, artists and critics answered the question of meaning with various kinds of interpretations.

Some saw the traditional metaphors, such as family, nature, or machine, as inferior or too limiting; art should be its own metaphor. Others claimed that nonrepresentational works were the most fitting expression for the communication of feeling and spirit. Many persons in search of "meaning" simply accepted an eroded confidence in their ability to understand "art"; no one denied its great importance. In fact, museums grew rapidly in the postwar period, and for city dwellers the trip to the museum on Sunday had overtones of a religious pilgrimage to a sacred site. Perhaps the mysterious and little understood forms of "art" contributed to the sanctification of the museum spaces. Meanwhile the age of television had begun, and this new medium appropriated many of the old myths and metaphors that nonrepresentational artists had discarded. The television screen began to be a conveyor of public, easily understood, visual symbols.

Since the triumph of nonrepresentational art at mid-century, many other styles have paraded across the critical horizon: Pop, Op, Super Realism, Conceptual Art, Anti-art, Objectless Art, and so on. In view of the rapidity of changing fashions, the notion of the avant garde has become meaningless.[28] While these styles have become familiar to the public through museums and magazines, most of these movements are preoccupied with private, rather than public, symbols. The hermetic nature of some of today's so-called high art frequently bears a strange resemblance to medieval alchemy.

Ironically, in the last decades of this century the most difficult forms to understand, the nonrepresentational, are the ones that now seem to dominate public spaces. Great abstract structures grace public parks and shopping malls, and large, nonmetaphorical, colored canvases adorn the walls of banks and business offices. The "meaning" of such nonrepresentational works depends heavily on caption and context. A nonrepresentational sculpture in a mall may be considered by the public merely decoration; in a museum it would be contemplated with all the dignity art deserves; in a chapel it becomes a sanctified object, creating a psychological mood in which to contemplate the holy. It is also likely that the artists who created such works would have their own private interpretations.

As we approach the end of the twentieth century the mass media, especially television, have emerged as major conveyors of public symbols. Television has woven a web of myths, furnishing the rhythms, the visual extravaganzas, and pseudo-liturgical seasons that break up the ordinariness of our lives. It is a primary source of orientation to the social, political, and economic spheres of experience. Although television may have its greatest impact on those who rely on it as a primary source of news and entertainment, its environment of symbols surrounds us all.

The basic task of this book has been, through analogies between older and newer symbolic forms of communication, to make connections between earlier American symbols and those of contemporary culture. One assumption that has shaped the task is a concept of what it means to be human — to be impelled by a desire to be a part of a transcendent whole that is larger than any creature, and, at the same time, to stand out as something different, something set apart. Images can and do symbolize concretely these human aspirations, not just for the artist alone, but for the whole community. When artists and religionists become immersed in private symbols, popular piety will find other forms in which to express faith.

Also central to this book is the assumption that human beings are sacramental creatures. The word *sacramental* in this context is used in a broad sense to emphasize that images, objects, and human gestures communicate in ways that words cannot. Visual forms of icon and ritual, thus, are not subservient to the word, but are important ways of mediating faith.[29] While visual symbols cannot perform the complex descriptive functions of language, their power to evoke feeling is unrivaled. To put these forms aside is to deny whole dimensions of human communication. This sacramental assumption has its roots in human existence: we are both flesh and spirit. Spirit cannot, in this world at least, be defleshed, disembodied, or dehumanized. Nor can flesh be despiritualized. Theologies and faiths that confine their expression to the word, written or spoken, and to music have issued an invitation to secular culture to minister to the sacramental needs of people. Secular culture is popular, not because it is secular, but perhaps because it is sacramental.

Through the ritual and iconic richness of its visual images, television answers, at least in part, those sacramental needs. Its images offer the security of real or imagined "worlds" larger than the individual. And at the same time they hold out to viewers, perhaps not the reality of heroism, but the excitement of vicarious human adventure. To live today in the awareness of a mystical, transcendent order of being and of unknown dimensions of time and human experience opens up fearful and undreamed-of worlds. These realities are frightening, for they awaken us from a sleep we had not known as sleep. It is much easier to pull the covers of culture over our heads and sleep a little longer before awakening. It is much easier to watch the world turn on soaps and stay tuned to the Super Bowl.

But it is also true that the shadowy myths of culture do satisfy our desire for community and for challenge. Unanswered is the question: Through what forms are religious traditions currently communicating the really great adventure? Until they can quicken the sensations of risk and challenge that animate the last nineteen seconds of a championship playoff with goal to go, the illusions of culture will continue to satisfy our need for belonging and wonder. Until institutional religion can excite the serious play of the soul and evoke the fullness of human passion, television will nurture our illusions of heroism and self-transcendence.

Notes

Introduction

1. Max Weber, *The Sociology of Religion* (Boston: Beacon Press, 1964), p. 117.

Chapter I: Ritual

1. W. E. H. Stanner, "The Dreaming," *Reader in Comparative Religion, An Anthropological Approach*, eds. William A. Lessa and Evon Z. Vogt (Evanston, Ill. & Elmsford, N.Y.: Row, Peterson and Company, 1958), p. 518.

2. *Myth* and *ritual* are terms used and interpreted, sometimes very differently, by scholars in a variety of disciplines. Some scholars see myth and ritual as two different forms of ordering experience. Given the independence of symbolic expression, myth can be objectified in different kinds of literary and artistic works. Other scholars, by contrast, maintain that myth and ritual are essentially correlative. They emphasize that myth is most authentic and visual when enacted in ritual. Myth comes to life in ritual, and communicants live in the myth through ritual experience. Whether in literary form or actualized in ritual, myths express dimensions of human experience that do not lend themselves to scientific verification. They are the proper expression of what Eric Voegelin refers to as the "blind spot" in human experience, the mystery of the beginning and the beyond. (See Eric Voegelin, *Order and History*, vol. 1 [Baton Rouge: Louisiana State University Press, 1956], p. 2.)

3. Johan Huizinga, *Homo Ludens: A Study of the Play-Element in Culture* (Boston: Beacon Press, 1955), pp. 26–27.

4. Hugo Rahner, *Man at Play* (New York: Herder and Herder, 1972), pp. 8, 10.

5. Victor Turner, "Process, System and Symbol: A New Anthropological Approach," *Daedalus*, Summer 1977, p. 61. "My personal view is that anthropology is shifting from a stress on concepts such as structure, equilibrium, function, system to process, indeterminacy, reflexivity — from a 'being' to a 'becoming' vocabulary."

6. Heb. 11:1.

7. Discussions with Aidan Kavanagh, O.S.B., professor of liturgics, the Divinity School, Yale University, were especially helpful in making comparisons, and contrasts between traditional rituals and substitutes for them in contemporary life.

8. Mircea Eliade, *Myth and Reality* (New York: Harper and Row, 1963), pp. 140–141.

9. Herbert J. Gans, *Deciding What's News* (New York: Random House, 1979), p. 298.

10. Ibid., p. 299.

11. Roland A. Delattre, "The Rituals of Humanity and the Rhythm of Reality," *Prospects: An Annual of American Studies* 5 (1979).

12. WNET/Thirteen, Transcript from *The MacNeil/Lehrer Report*, "The Massachusetts and Vermont Primaries," air date: March 5, 1980, p. 7.

13. Ibid.

14. Martin Linsky, "The System's Working Just Fine," *Boston Globe*, March 12, 1980, p. 15.

15. Philip L. Geyelin, "New Technology and the Evolution of Politics," *Yale Alumni Magazine and Journal*, January 1979, p. 12.

Chapter II: Icon

1. There are differences in the meaning of the term in Eastern Orthodoxy and Western Christian thought. For a very clear statement about the nature and significance of the icon in Eastern Orthodoxy see Chapter I, "The Orthodox Icon," in Ernst Benz, *The Eastern Orthodox Church* (New York: Anchor Books, 1963). Icons in the Eastern tradition were not simply representations but were "manifestations of the heavenly archetypes." The countenances of Christ, of the Blessed Virgin, or of a saint were therefore true epiphanies, self-made imprints of the celestial archetype and inspired a reciprocal relationship between viewer and image. "In Byzantium the beholder was not kept at a distance from the image: he entered within its aura of sanctity, and the image, in turn, partook of the space in which he moved. He was not so much a 'beholder' as a 'participant.' While it does not aim at illusion, Byzantine religious art abolished all clear distinction between the world of reality and the world of appearance." (p. 4)

   In the Western Catholic tradition images did not have this same kind of identity with the prototype. The emphasis was placed on representation and narrative, rather than presentation of the sacred through the image. For an excellent analysis of the differences between the Eastern and Western Catholic traditions, see Edwyn Bevan, *Holy Images* (London: George Allen & Unwin, 1940). In the Western Latin tradition, homage passes through the material symbols to the persons for whom the symbol stands. (p. 152) The controversy of images in Western theology has centered on the ontological status of the material symbol itself and the relationship between the image and its archetype. As long as no supernatural power is thought to be residing in images, the use of images to call up recollections, ideas, or emotions is acceptable even among some Protestants. (p. 169) However, the Catholic traditions, both East and West, have made the greatest use of sacred images, although their interpretations of the status and the homage due the image differ. While the distinctions are very complex, often confusing, Bevan concludes that "images in the Latin West have never had the place in religion which wonder-working icons have had in Greek and Russian Christianity." (p. 157) As Bevan observes, the controversial question is whether or not the images are charged with a quasipersonal supernatural power. (p. 177)

2. Horace Newcomb, "Assessing the Violence Profile Studies of Gerbner and Gross, A Humanistic Critique and Suggestion," *Communication Research*, 5, no. 3 (July 1978): 280.

3. Two scholars, Robert Alley and Irby Brown, are currently engaged in a systematic study of the history and development of family images in television. This research will be published in a forthcoming book.

4. Arnold Hano, "Enough Is Enough," *TV Guide*, October 29, 1977, pp. 14–15.

5. Ibid., p. 15.

6. Michael J. Arlen, "Smooth Pebbles at Southfork," *The New Yorker*, March 24, 1980, p. 118.

7. Neil Shister, "Soap Operas Are Real," *Boston Globe*, August 7, 1978, Living Section, p. 14.

8. Ibid.

9. Thomas Cole, "Essay on American Scenery," *American Monthly*, 1 n.s. (1836): 1–12.

10. Nathalia Wright, *Horatio Greenough: The First American Sculptor* (Philadelphia: University of Pennsylvania Press, 1963), p. 161.

11. John Cawelti, *The Six-Gun Mystique* (Bowling Green, Ohio: Bowling Green University Popular Press, 1975), p. 38.

12. Horace Newcomb, *TV: The Most Popular Art* (Garden City, N.Y.: Anchor Press, 1974), p. 68.

13. Cawelti, p. 59.

14. Horatio Greenough, *Form and Function: Remarks on Art, Design and Architecture*, ed. Harold A. Small (Berkeley: University of California Press, 1962), p. 57.

15. Ibid., pp. 60–61.

16. Ibid., p. 118.

17. Frank Lloyd Wright, "The Art and Craft of the Machine," in *Frank Lloyd Wright: Writings and Buildings* (New York: Horizon, 1969), p. 55.

18. Constance M. Rourke, *Charles Sheeler: Artist in the American Tradition* (New York: Harcourt Brace and Co., 1938), p. 130.

19. "CHIPs," *TV Guide*, September 10, 1977, p. 59.

20. Advertisement in *TV Guide*, March 5, 1980, p. A–98.

Chapter III: Iconoclasm

1. Edwyn Bevan, *Holy Images* (London: George Allen and Unwin, 1940), pp. 29–30.

2. For a long time it was believed that Judaism strictly adhered to this prohibition of images in places of worship. But the excavations at Dura-Europus, a third-century Jewish synagogue, testified to the narrative use of images. On the walls were found paintings that depicted the Exodus from Egypt, the miraculous well at Beer, the vision of Ezekiel, and other memorable events from Jewish sacred his-

tory. One wall also contained a niche, apparently for the Torah; this was surrounded by large painted figures of heroes of the faith such as Abraham and Moses. Throughout these wall paintings the activity of God is represented at the top of each narrative sequence by a hand that seems to break into human history at critical points. For an account of this excavation and interpretation of the paintings, see Carl H. Kraeling, *The Excavations at Dura-Europus, Sixth Season* (New Haven: Yale University Press, 1932–33), and M. Rostovtseff, *Dura-Europus and Its Art* (Oxford, England: Clarendon Press, 1938).

3. While the major arguments against the use of images in religious spaces have been theological, there have been others with a different rationale. The great medieval churchman, Bernard of Clairvaux, was very critical of images in the sanctuary, and his complaints were liturgical and ethical. The sculptured capitals at Vézelay that narrate biblical stories came under his fierce critical scrutiny. For him, these visible forms, unlike words or music, were a deterrent to spiritual reflection. To this criticism St. Bernard also added an ethical reason for banishing images. Why, he asked, if they could not see them as distracting, could they not see such sculpture as an unnecessary love of possessions and worldly luxury? It would be better, he advised, to use the money spent on such ornamentation to feed the poor. In his own order, the Cistercian, church architecture was emphatically simple and functional.

These convictions — theological, liturgical, and ethical — which advocated the rejection of images in sacred spaces, have, in fact, led to an aniconic, or iconless, aesthetic in art and architecture. It is an aesthetic that emphasizes the beauty of simple geometric and functional forms and materials. The grandeur of Cistercian churches, for example, comes from proportionality, space, shapes, and lights. Careful ordering and scaling of interrelated functional parts produce a visual choreography of abstract geometrical shapes enhanced by the light. Naves are devoid of any imagery, and sunlight, coming in through clear glass windows, sets up rhythms of shadows on plain stone surfaces of walls and piers. A similar aniconic aesthetic appears in early church building in the Protestant sectors of American culture. The Shakers, referred to in Chapter II, shared this aniconic aesthetic with the Cistercians.

4. Nast cartoon reproduced in Morton Keller, *The Art and Politics of Thomas Nast* (New York: Oxford University Press, 1968), illus. no. 99. Original illustration dated October 1, 1870.

5. Illustration in *The Masses*, 5, no. 1, issue no. 29 (October 1913): 18.

6. Judith Mara Gutman, *Lewis W. Hine* (New York: Walker and Co., 1967), p. 19.

7. Ibid., p. 79.

8. William Stott, *Documentary Expression and Thirties America* (New York: Oxford University Press, 1973), pp. 6, 7.

9. Ibid., p. 20.

10. Introductory essay by George P. Elliott, *Dorothea Lange* (New York: Museum of Modern Art, 1966), p. 103.

11. Ben Shahn, *The Shape of Content* (Cambridge: Harvard University Press, 1957), p. 110.

12. Quote accompanies photograph entitled "Iwo Jima, 1945," which appears in *W. Eugene Smith* (New York: Museum of Modern Art, 1970).

13. Paul Rotha, "Some Principles of Documentary," *Non Fiction Film Theory and Criticism*, ed. Richard Meram Barsam (New York: E. P. Dutton & Co., 1976), p. 51.

14. Erik Barnouw, *Documentary: A History of the Non-Fiction Film* (New York: Oxford University Press, 1974), p. 139.

15. Erik Barnouw, *Tube of Plenty: The Evolution of American Television* (New York: Oxford University Press, 1975), p. 171.

16. Ibid., p. 175.

17. Ibid., pp. 176–177.

18. Ibid., p. 179.

19. Ibid., p. 180.

20. Jack Gould, "The Unselling of the Pentagon," *New York Times*, March 7, 1971.

21. Michael J. Robinson, "Public Affairs Television and the Growth of Political Malaise: The Case of 'The Selling of the Pentagon,' " *American Political Science Review* 70 (1976): 414–415.

22. Ibid., p. 417.

23. Ernest Becker, *The Denial of Death* (New York: The Free Press, 1975), p. x.

24. Barnouw, *Tube of Plenty*, pp. 455–456.

25. WNET/TV, Transcript of *The Adversaries*, March 28, 1974, p. 15.

26. Barnouw, *Tube of Plenty*, p. 384.

27. Transcript of *The Adversaries*, p. 7

28. Ibid.

29. E. H. Gombrich, "The Visual Image," *Scientific American*, 227, no. 3 (September 1972): 82.

30. Conversations with David Thorburn, author of forthcoming book, *Story Machine*, were particularly helpful in considering the role of comedians in iconoclastic television.

31. Neil Hickey, "Is Television Doing Its Investigative Reporting Job?," *TV Guide*, April 2, 1977, p. 4.

32. John Culhane, "Where Documentaries Don't Dare to Tread," *New York Times*, February 20, 1977, Section 2.

33. Letter to the Editor in John Sharnik, "More on the TV Taboos," *New York Times*, Section 2.

34. Culhane, "Where Documentaries," Section 2.

35. Ibid.

36. Ibid.

37. Ibid.

Chapter IV: TV

1. Peter L. Berger and Thomas Luckmann, *The Social Construction of Reality* (Garden City, N.Y.: Anchor Press/Doubleday, 1967), p. 98.

2. Ibid., p. 99.

3. Peter L. Berger, *A Rumor of Angels* (Garden City, N.Y.: Anchor Press/Doubleday, 1970), p. 52.

4. H. Richard Niebuhr, *Radical Monotheism and Western Culture* (New York: Harper and Brothers, 1960), p. 16.

5. Ibid., p. 17.

6. Becker's use of the word *illusion* can be a stumbling block to readers who do not abandon its usual negative connotations — "delusion," "deception," "unreality," "error." His concept of illusion can best be compared to Johan Huizinga's concept of play, and he himself makes the connection. "As we have learned from Huizinga . . . the only secure truth [men and women] have is that which they themselves create and dramatize; to live is to play at the meaning of life." (p. 201) Far from being a reductionist,

Becker places the symbolic activity and the search for meaning at the center of human endeavors.

7. Becker, *The Denial of Death.*

8. Ibid., p. 200.

9. These observations were made at a Rockefeller Consultation, "Reporting on Religious News in the Media," June 13, 1980, during an informal discussion of ritualistic dimensions in television news.

10. Rockefeller Consultation, June 13, 1980. Comments made during discussion of television news reporting.

11. Such a tendency of persons to appropriate news media as a source of collective symbols and participation is not new with the medium of television. Alexis de Tocqueville, the nineteenth-century French observer of American life and politics, saw, even then, the capacity of the press in a democratic, voluntaristic society to become a unifying force that could identify a collective whole. Writing long before the electronic age, de Tocqueville's comments about the newspaper would be applicable today, especially to television:

> A newspaper is an adviser that does not require to be sought, but that comes of its own accord and talks to you briefly every day on the common weal, without distracting you from your private affairs.

De Tocqueville observed that in a democratic country a great number of persons who want to combine cannot do so because they are scattered, very insignificant, and lost amid the crowd. They cannot see and do not know how to find one another. He saw the power of newspapers to furnish symbols of the group and its action with which individuals could identify. To that power television news has added a ritualistic dimension by its rhythmic, daily images of sights and sounds seen simultaneously by millions of viewers. Were de Tocqueville alive today, he could say, as he did of newspapers: Television brought them together, and it is necessary to keep them united.

> All are then immediately guided towards this
> beacon; and these wandering minds, which
> had long sought each other in darkness, at
> length meet and unite.

But it is important also to add that de Tocqueville saw connections between the number of public associations and the number of newspapers in this country. The subdivisions of political power, the multiplicity of associations and newspapers indicated to him the "utmost national freedom combined with local freedom of every kind." His closing reflections on the press are especially relevant for us today. "The more equal the conditions of men become and the less strong men individually are, the more easily they give way to the current of the multitude and the more difficult it is for them to adhere . . . to an opinion which the multitude discards." Newspapers and, I might add, television address readers and viewers in the name of all others, and can exert an influence over persons in proportion to their individual weaknesses. Alexis de Tocqueville, "On the Relation Between Public Associations and the Newspapers," in *Democracy in America*, vol. 2, book 2, ed. P. Bradley (New York: Vintage Books, 1958), pp. 119–122.

12. Becker, *Denial of Death*, pp. 150–152.

13. Niebuhr, *Radical Monotheism and Western Culture*, p. 118.

14. Margaret Mead, "The American Family: An Endangered Species?," *TV Guide*, December 30, 1978.

15. A Report of the United States Commission on Civil Rights, *Window Dressing on the Set: Women and Minorities in*

Television (Washington, D.C.: U.S. Government Printing Office, August 1977), p. 41.

16. "Television's New Primetime Man," *Ebony*, December 1979, p. 128.

17. *Window Dressing*, pp. 71–72.

18. A Report of the United States Commission on Civil Rights, *Window Dressing on the Set: An Update* (Washington, D.C.: U.S. Government Printing Office, January 1979), pp. 20–22.

19. We become aware of the contrast between questions raised through our cultural symbols and those of others when we look at essential questions that appear in philosophy and in certain religious traditions. The shallowness of our cultural questions shows up when persons recall experiential human questions. Historian and philosopher Eric Voegelin has observed that these questions are rooted in the openness of existence and can "result in such metaphysical questions as the fundamental ones formulated by Leibniz: Why is there something and not nothing? Why is something as it is and not different? There is a question that is inherent in existence. These are the fundamental questions of experience to which there *is* no answer." "Questions Up," in *Conversations with Eric Voegelin*, Papers of the Thomas More Institute, 1976, p. 103.

20. Jacques Ellul, *Propaganda* (New York: Random House/Vintage, 1973), pp. 62ff.

21. Ibid., p. 65.

22. Ibid., p. 68.

23. Harry J. Skornia, *Television and Society* (New York: McGraw-Hill, 1965), p. 151.

24. Ibid.

25. Ibid., p. 145.

26. For a discussion of changing technology in communications and subsequent problems of freedom and control, see John Wicklein, *The New Communications and Freedom*, to be published by Viking Press in 1981.

27. In the twentieth century, some artists have self-consciously fashioned an imageless aesthetic outside of particular religious institutions. Early in this century artists began to eliminate narrative or representational subjects and to experiment with compositions of shapes and colors that bore no likeness to ordinary visual perceptions of the physical world. There were two dominant sources of early modern imageless painting and sculpture. One was identified with a deliberate rejection of material objects and a quest for abstract visual forms which would best symbolize spirituality. A second source of abstraction was the search of artists who, rather than reject the material world, delved deeper into matter to discover the essential structures of *soma*, and even spirit.

    Wassily Kandinsky (1866–1944) was among the first artists to reject material objects as subject matter for paintings. His work and theories have stimulated discussions and experiments throughout this century. Although he drew many of his concepts of spirituality from theosophy, his aniconic aesthetic evolved from his own investigations, rather than from the collective efforts of a religious community such as the Cistercians or Shakers. Yet, while he did not produce paintings for liturgical settings, his ideas are not unlike those encountered in traditional religious arguments against the use of images. Kandinsky, for example, in his book, *Concerning the Spiritual in Art* (published in the United States in 1914), spoke about the need for reform and purification of art forms in view of the materialism of Western culture. Most important, in his paintings he experimented with imageless forms and colors he considered most fitting for the communication of invisible spiritual realities. Of special interest to later-twentieth-century viewers is Kandinsky's desire to find a means of universal visual communication. Nonrepresentational compositions of colors and shapes had, he believed, a revelatory power which, like music, could transcend cultural boundaries and express the invisible life of the spirit to all persons. Imageless art for Kandinsky would lead to a larger social and moral role of the artist in modern society.

Some American artists were also experimenting with nonrepresentational forms at this time. As early as 1910 the painter Arthur G. Dove (1880–1946) had done a series of small paintings with no recognizable subject matter. But Dove's motivation toward abstraction differed from Kandinsky's. The source of Dove's abstraction was the distillation of natural forms, and his attitude toward the highly simplified shapes and colors was ambiguous. Shortly after these early experiments with seemingly imageless paintings he remarked to the photographer Alfred Steiglitz that he had to return to nature to keep his work vital. Throughout his career the shapes in Dove's paintings hovered between highly abstracted natural forms and imageless ones. In some of his works viewers can identify simplified elemental images — sun, sea, earth. Other paintings have only ambiguous, organic shapes and depend upon titles, such as *Life Goes On*, to suggest the earth forms and growth patterns. Rather than polarize matter and spirit, Dove probed nature to discover essential structures, and he used these to visualize the invisible, mysterious life force that animates material existence. Paradoxically, Dove's work both is and is not aniconic. Much of it appears at first glance to be imageless, but the abstractions evolved from his concentration upon natural forms.

In the 1940s and 1950s there were distinct shifts in the motivation and interpretation of imageless painting and sculpture. Some painters and critics denounced communication of any kind, either public or private. The imageless painting or sculpture was devoid of meaning; it was autonomous in itself, and "meaning" attributed to it was an adulteration of "pure" form. Many painters and critics viewed imageless art as the expression of private realities or feelings. In the absence of commonly perceived visual references critics provided a great variety of interpretive frameworks for these imageless works. Suzanne Langer, for example, in an essay, "The Art Symbol and the Symbol in Art" (*Problems of Art: Ten Philosophical Lectures* by Suzanne K. Langer. New York: Scribners, 1957), speculated that the abstract clusters of pigments were as close as one could get to the raw emotion of the artist. Other critics found clues to the meaning of aniconic works in the personality or expressed concerns of an artist. Barnett Newman's interest in mysticism and some titles of his paintings led many interpreters to use the word *religious* to describe his work. Art critic Harold Rosenberg (*New Yorker*, January 1, 1972, p. 46) observed, however, that Newman's readings provided insight only into the atmosphere that surrounded his mental operations. Ultimately, it was not really certain what the "rectangles and zips mean." Rosenberg concluded that painting was for Newman a way of "practicing" the sublime, not "conveying" it.

The general public came to accept imageless art, as well as all the subsequent isms and fashions that followed, as something they needed help from critics in understanding. Along with that acceptance, however, came the unexamined presupposition that today artists have no responsibility for communicating shared public symbols. This shift in the perception of the role of art and artists has, in turn, nurtured the concept that "art," with or without recognizable images, is primarily understood by artists and critics. This concept is abandoned from time to time when museums feature the great treasures of the past — Egyptian, Celtic, Roman, and so on. Thousands rush to the museum and everyone is pleased: artists, critics, museum staffs, general public. Such exhibitions recall for us the role of art as conveyor of the shared symbols of a society.

28. James Ackerman, "The Demise of the Avant Garde," *L'Arte* 6 (1969): 4–11. In this article, Ackerman points out that in a society committed to novelty the role of the avant garde has been abolished. "In a dynamic society committed to an expanding economy, technology, education, and welfare, continuing innovation is a condition of survival, and one that can be taken for granted. The artist, critic, and historian can afford to focus attention on problems of value and meaning."

29. The word *sacramental* can refer, of course, to some specific kinds of meditation of grace. There are complex histories of interpretations of particular sacraments in Roman Catholicism and Protestantism; these include intricate doctrinal and dogmatic controversies about the nature of particular sacraments and their capacity to infuse grace. The specific theological questions of the salvific efficacy of this or that sacrament is not the issue here. I have introduced the word *sacramental* to direct readers to an essential issue that precedes the others: the capacity of materiality to embody spirit or the mystery of grace.

Index